Small Steps Forward

by the same author

Stepping Out
Using Games and Activities to Help Your Child with Special Needs
Sarah Newman
ISBN 978 1 84310 110 9

of related interest

Playing, Laughing and Learning with Children on the Autism Spectrum
A Practical Resource of Play Ideas for Parents and Carers
Second Edition
Julia Moor
ISBN 978 1 84310 608 1

Fun with Messy Play
Ideas and Activities for Children with Special Needs
Tracey Beckerleg
ISBN 978 1 84310 641 8

Autism, Play and Social Interaction
Lone Gammeltoft and Marianne Sollok Nordenhof
Translated by Erik van Acker
ISBN 978 1 84310 520 6

Replays
Using Play to Enhance Emotional and Behavioral Development for
Children with Autism Spectrum Disorders
Karen Levine and Naomi Chedd
ISBN 978 1 84310 832 0

Narrative Approaches in Play with Children
Ann Cattanach
ISBN 978 1 84310 588 6

Practical Sensory Programmes for Students with Autism Spectrum
Disorder and Other Special Needs
Sue Larkey
ISBN 978 1 84310 479 7

Everyday Education
Visual Support for Children with Autism
Pernille Dyrbjerg and Maria Vedel
Foreword by Lennart Pedersen
ISBN 978 1 84310 457 5

Small Steps Forward

Using Games and Activities to Help Your Pre-School Child with Special Needs

SARAH NEWMAN

ILLUSTRATED BY JEANIE MELLERSH

SECOND EDITION

Jessica Kingsley Publishers
London and Philadelphia

First published in 2008
by Jessica Kingsley Publishers
116 Pentonville Road
London N1 9JB, UK
and
400 Market Street, Suite 400
Philadelphia, PA 19106, USA

www.jkp.com

Library of Congress Cataloging in Publication Data
Newman, Sarah, 1963-
    Small steps forward : using games and activities to help your pre-school child with special needs /
Sarah Newman ; illustrated by Jeanie Mellersh. -- 2nd ed.
        p. cm.
    Includes bibliographical references and index.
    ISBN 978-1-84310-693-7 (pb)
        1. Children with disabilities--Education (Preschool) 2. Developmentally disabled children--Educa-
tion (Preschool) 3. Education, Preschool--Activity programs. 4. Educational games. 5. Child development. I. Title.
    LC4019.2.N48 2008
    371.9'0472--dc22

                                                                    2008005851

British Library Cataloguing in Publication Data
A CIP catalogue record for this book is available from the British Library

ISBN 978 1 84310 693 7

Printed and bound in the United States by
Thomson-Shore, 7300 Joy Road, Dexter, MI 48130

This book is dedicated
to my son Christopher.

Contents

Acknowledgements

I would like to thank the following for their help: Bernie and daughter Claire Barratt; Katherine and children Christopher and Alice Bowell; Lisa and son Jordan Burnell; Tracey and daughter Jade Burrows; Clare and niece Lauren Cooper; Suzannah and Mike and son Daniel Fussell; Sarah and son James Hicks; Liz and son Andrew Hiscox; Richard and Elizabeth and daughter Natasha Jay; Shirley and son Mikey Jones; Peter and son Sebastian Jung; Cheryl and son Alan Maher; Lisa and son Warren Muggleton; Julie and son Liam Ockelford; Julie and son Sam Pursey; Karen and daughter Katy Spurway; Sharon and daughter Georgina Street; Jacolyn and son Declan Thomas; Liz and son Jonathan Washbourn; Lucy and son Jedd Waterton; Jackie and daughter Emily Whitley; Diedre and son Oliver Witherby; Julie and Tom and daughter Alice Wood.

I would also like to thank the following for giving their professional advice: Ann Baker, Joan Turnbull Opportunity Group; Jasia Beaumont, Sleep Clinic Nurse; Jane Davey, Citizens Advice Bureau; Jane Dutton, Hardmoor Early Years Centre; Lucinda Edwards, Avon Valley Opportunity Group; Caroline Evans, Portage Home Visitor; Sue Evans, Social Worker; Emma Gibbs, Educational Psychologist; Dr Neil Harris, Consultant Child Psychiatrist; Dr Jo Lee, GP; Ally Levell, Joan Turnbull Opportunity Group; Ingrid Marcham, Joan Turnbull Opportunity Group; Liz Matthew, Occupational Therapist; Irene Osman, Swimming Instructor; Jenny Powell, Occupational Therapist; David Reid, Parent Partnership Service, Hampshire County Council; Lyn Rollison, Portage Home Visitor; Dr Carolyn Smith, Educational Psychologist; Dr Kara Tanaga, GP; Katrina Watt, Fortune Centre of Riding Therapy and Cynthia Wilson, Music Teacher.

I would like to thank the Makaton Vocabulary Development Project for allowing me to reproduce the signs and symbols for cat and biscuit on p.103.

I would like to thank all the children, some with special needs and some without, who modelled for the illustrations in the book.

My very special thanks are due to the following who gave me so much time and help: Pam Gammer, Senior Portage Home Visitor; Sally Goodson, Speech and Language Therapist; Katya Gorman, Occupational Therapist; Jenny Gurd, Supervisor, Joan Turnbull Opportunity Group; Kenzie Revington, Physiotherapist and Dr Valerie Shrubb FRCPCH, Consultant Paediatrician.

For the second edition I was helped by many old friends who are listed above and many others. I would particularly like to thank Rebecca Fox, Barbara Humphreys, Jacky Lewis, Denise Phillips and Rosie Mitchell.

I would also like to thank Sharon Brien, Jacky Donnellan, Jenny Ladbury, Jo Strudwick, my brother James and my parents who all helped in different ways. I would like to thank Jeanie Mellersh for her wonderful illustrations. She was a constant source of ideas, encouragement and support. Thanks also to Nick Mellersh for all his help. Above all I would like to thank David for all his help and encouragement.

Preface

Just before Christopher's first birthday we took him to see a paediatrician because he was failing to reach his developmental milestones. We were told that he was developmentally delayed and that he would need all sorts of tests, including genetic tests and a brain scan to see if a diagnosis could be reached. We were fortunate that Christopher started at an Opportunity Group within a week and that eventually he received all sorts of help including portage, riding, speech and occupational therapy. I find it impossible to think back to that time without remembering the utter desperation, despair and inadequacy my partner David and I felt at the news and in the months to come. Christopher was our first child and the pregnancy and birth had seemed to go well. Christopher was slow to develop but we thought it was just that – slowness – and had not imagined that he had serious developmental problems. Looking back now, having had two more sons – Nicholas and William – I can see that Christopher was different from birth, but that is another story. At one Christopher couldn't sit up, he didn't make eye contact and rarely showed any interest in anything or anybody apart from a set of keys.

Having discovered there was a problem, I wanted to find out what I could do to help him develop and move on. I looked for books but could not find anything that addressed very early skills in an approachable way. Christopher had no diagnosis so it was difficult to tap into the different organizations around. In the end, I just badgered different professionals to give me suggestions – work on eye contact, work on object permanence etc. It helped me to feel I was doing something and it certainly helped him. From about 20 months he started to make real progress and has continued to do so to date. I pay tribute to the many professionals who in the early days found time to talk and help despite busy schedules, particularly Pam Gammer (portage home visitor) and

Jenny Gurd (Opportunity Group Supervisor). I don't know what I would have done without them.

One day, just before Christopher was three, Pam unloaded her bag of toys in the sitting room and out tumbled some books on games for children. She said that one of her 'mums' wanted some ideas for games, so she had found some books for ordinary children which she could use by adapting the games to a more appropriate level. It was at that moment that the idea came to me of writing a book for parents of children with special needs, the kind of book that I had sought and been unable to find. It would show how development proceeded so that parents would know where their child is and where he or she is heading. I also wanted to produce a book which wasn't specific to a certain condition because problems often span a number of developmental areas and many young children don't have a diagnosis. Shortly after my starting to write this book, however, Christopher received the diagnosis of autism.

Ten years on, there is a multitude of material on the market and early diagnosis is more common. However, this book has had an enduring popularity with parents because it is positive, accessible, easy to dip into and reflects their real lives. This second edition has enabled me to rewrite the last two chapters so they are up to date and reflect current practice. Whilst much of child development remains the same, I have been able to incorporate new developments such as PECS (Picture Exchange Communication System) and sensory integration which will be of even greater benefit to young children with special needs.

How the book is structured

Ordinary children are programmed to learn and develop. They are always investigating and exploring while they play and are always processing the information they discover to make sense of the world. They are responsive, interested, motivated and endlessly creative, constantly testing and assimilating what they have learnt. They have the means and the motivation to be constantly moving forward and they can demand from adults the support and information they need.

For children with special needs it is often not so easy. In one way or another you have to give them more help and encouragement, whether it is stimulation, motivation, information or support. In some development areas you have to introduce the next step, extending your children's play and helping them with specific problems. Therefore you have to have an understanding of their developmental stage and what you expect them to do next so that you can help them move forward in small steps to reach their full potential.

The book has been written to give you an idea of the progression of child development so you can see where your child is and where he or she is heading. It starts off with how to cope with having a child with special needs and then moves on to give general advice on how to play with your child. The core of the book divides child development into the following areas: cognitive, language, physical, sensory, social and emotional, because these are the most easily understood. However, these divisions are somewhat artificial. All areas of development are inter-related and therefore there is a lot of repetition of skills like turn-taking, object permanence and copying, which are relevant to more than one area.

Each chapter takes one developmental area, describes a child's progression, and then suggests a variety of games and activities to help stimulate the child along the way. The child's progression is further subdivided into chronological development which describes the order in which skills are gained and parallel development for those skills which develop continuously alongside each other.

Following this, Chapter 9, Everyday Living, gives information on tackling the issues of behaviour management, sleep and toileting. Chapter 10, The Support Your Child Should Expect, gives information on the support that is available from health, education and social services in your child's early years, choosing a pre-school and school for your child, the statutory assessment process and sources of financial support. Chapter 11, Resources, gives ideas if you require further information including a bibliography and addresses of voluntary organizations.

How to use this book

I have not written this book to tell you what you **should** be doing with your child. It is only to give you some ideas of games if you **want** to do something more structured. In no way do I want to make you feel any more pressure. There will be many times when you just want to have fun with your child in a completely free way. On those occasions you should leave this book on the shelf.

Don't read this book in one go. Read Chapter 1, How to Survive, if you need to. Then read Chapter 2, What Everyone Needs to Know, and the sections which are relevant to your child. If you read it all you will probably just feel overwhelmed. It is not designed to cover one moment in time but to cover years of development. Concentrate on the sections which are relevant to your child at a particular time and then look again in a few months time as your child develops.

Remember that not all the ideas will work for all children or every disability. Use and adapt what you think will work for your child.

I have deliberately not put any reference to the age at which children are expected to achieve skills. Such age guidelines are vague – just compare the different skills of a group of one-year-olds. I believe that it is important for parents to be aware of the progress their child is making, however small, but it does not help to make comparisons with their child's peers. If you do want to know, there are many excellent books which give indications of ages. See the bibliography in Chapter 11, Resources.

This book is inevitably a starting point if you find your child has special needs and you want to do something constructive in the first few months and years. If in time you need more specialist information and advice, refer to the organizations and books listed in Chapter 11, Resources.

Please note

1. I have included quotes from parents about their experiences. Sometimes the child's name has been changed.

2. I have used the terms 'he' and 'she' interchangeably to represent your child.

3. I have written this book from the standpoint of a family consisting of a mother and father. However, I appreciate that this is not always the case, and hope that the many lone parents who may be reading this book will have no difficulty in adapting the ideas and activities to their circumstances.

4. When making toys or using household objects as toys, make sure they are safe and appropriate for your child.

5. If you are concerned about any area of your child's development seek advice from your health visitor or general practitioner. They should be able to help you or refer you to someone more appropriate.

CHAPTER 1

How to Survive

This section reflects how I have felt and how I have coped with my own situation but also draws on many of the experiences other parents have told me about. You may not recognize the emotions I talk about and may have found other ways of surviving. You may find it too recent and too raw. I wish I had known this when my child was diagnosed as having special needs but I suspect you have to live through it all to be able to feel this way.

First of all, parents have to admit that their child does have a problem. It can take many parents a long time before they can accept this.

For most parents it is a terrible shock when they find out they have a child with special needs. They experience a period of sadness and even desolation and desperation as they try to work through what it means now and for the future.

I felt totally and utterly destroyed by the news of Christopher's problems. I felt inadequate and unprepared. I felt guilty in case I was in some way responsible, I felt it was punishment for making glib assumptions about Christopher – 'when he goes to university', 'when he leaves home', etc. I had no idea what the future held for him – whether he would even walk or talk. I didn't know what the consequences would be for my partner and I – whether we could risk having any more children, whether we would always have a dependent and embarrassing son with us. All those happy, cosy, 'normal' assumptions had gone out of the window and I was left with an incredible sadness, a feeling of being totally alone, even though I have a wonderfully supportive partner and family, and a sense of inadequacy about facing the future and all its terrible uncertainties. And yet I still had this little chap who I loved and who was totally dependent on me and through it all I had to continue caring for him and I suppose that is the way I got through it – by looking after and loving my own child as he was and learning to take each day at a time.

Despite what people say, you never 'get over' finding out that your child has special needs. The hurt will always be with you and the problems and difficulties, though they may change, will always be present. However, most parents find a way of dealing with it on a daily basis and thereby come to some sort of acceptance of what it means for them and their child.

Coming to terms with your child's situation

Finding out that your child has special needs is a devastating experience which stays with you for the rest of your life. It never ceases to be with you and to affect everything you do and think about your child and everything else as well. Many people find themselves profoundly changed by the experience. On the negative side they are more bitter and angry but on the positive side more tolerant and aware and in tune with what is important in life.

> I felt I went through a kind of grieving process when I found my son had special needs – a mourning for a child I thought I had, for lost expectations, hopes and assumptions. Christopher was one year old when we found out he had significant problems and we didn't know if he would walk or talk, let alone go to the local school or leave home. It takes a long time to come to terms with your child's situation, to feel at ease with all the unknowns and able to move on to look to the future. I felt it took about six months before I was on a fairly even keel but even now, several years on, I still can get upset by memories, by seeing normal children doing normal things or by careless comments by other parents. The struggle of everyday life can also be overwhelming at times. I felt I changed. I make fewer assumptions about life and, I hope, am less judgemental and more accepting of people and situations.

Strategies

- Hold on to how much you **love your child**, how much he needs you and you him. Enjoy him. Think of him first as the child you want and love and second as someone with special needs.

> When I came back from hospital with Matthew after his diagnosis I remember thinking that there was no point talking to him because I thought that he was a 'vegetable'. The feeling lasted for a few hours only and then I was back in the instinctive role of loving and caring for my child. It is quite frightening to look back and see how negative I felt.

- **Take one day at a time** and don't try to look too far into the future. Deal with your child as he is now and will be in the next few days and weeks. Who knows what any child will be like five or ten years hence?

- **Move forward**. Concentrate on the improvements and the progress your child is making, however small, rather than any comparison with his peers.

How to stay sane

Having children is hard work and having children with special needs can be harder still. Parents have to provide a lot of care, maybe carrying out medical procedures, and they have to do a lot more hands-on playing. All this has to be incorporated into a busy day. Children with special needs often have behavioural problems which are stressful for their parents. Just carrying and moving children who are unable to walk is physically demanding and there is often extra washing and cleaning. Daily life is quickly taken up with appointments at hospitals, with therapists and getting to and from playgroups. Finally, there can be considerable stress both in negotiating with the professional services to get the best for a child now, and in contemplating what the future holds.

> I don't think it is generally recognized how hard things can be for parents of children with special needs. If you ask friends and family with children how they view their lives, they will tell you that their lives are tough. I know that when I found things very hard this response made me feel totally inadequate. Their lives were tough but they were coping, I wasn't. It was only later when I had another child that I realized that I wasn't inadequate and that life with a child with special needs is very different and very difficult.

Having children is hard work

Parents often don't get much positive encouragement. Friends and family rarely tell parents that they are doing a good job raising their children. If they are seen to cope then people assume they are okay and do not need support and encouragement. So the onus is largely on parents themselves to recognize when they need help and to demand it. Parents feel that they should be able to cope on their own, so when they do give in and ask for support they feel as if they have failed. Added to this, other parents often look askance when they hear of the support available, such as playgroups and respite care, and even tell parents of children with special needs how 'lucky they are'.

Strategies

- Resist attempts to be heroic. Be realistic. Remember that only you know your child, your circumstances and your needs. **Take any help you can get** from family, friends, social services etc. whether it is help in the house or respite care for your child. If you send your child to a childminder, make sure your child is secure and comfortable, that the childminder has confidence that she can understand and deal with your child's needs and that you feel totally happy with the arrangement. Start by leaving your child for an hour or so and build up to whatever you need. Find an arrangement that suits you. Your child could go to the carer's house or the carer could come to you if it makes you more comfortable. Your child will also benefit from the different experience, environment and people – so everyone wins.

- Seriously **consider any opportunities that are offered to your child** like a place at an Opportunity Group or Child Development Centre. These places can be frightening for parents because they force them to confront the fact that their child has special needs and that he may be placed with other children who have different and maybe more severe needs. However, if your child may benefit from the experience it is worth trying.

- **Find local networks of parents in similar situations**. There are many ways for parents to meet other parents who have faced similar experiences, for example through parent support groups, Child Development Centres or national organizations with local branches (see Chapter 11). Alternatively you can ask your doctors or therapists to help you make contact with parents of children with similar special needs. You probably won't like everyone you meet but if you make an effort you may make some good friends. It can be helpful and reassuring to meet parents who have been there before and survived. If you meet parents of children with the same or similar problems to yours you can also share useful information, concerns and ideas. If they are a bit further down the line with an older child they can give you an idea of future issues like schooling. (However, some parents find it disturbing to meet children much older than their own or with more severe problems.) It can also be much more relaxing visiting people whose children have special needs since they are more understanding of odd behaviour and their houses are often geared up more appropriately. Neither side feels they have to make constant excuses and apologies for their children.

- **Take time out for yourself**. Your own interests may not seem very important compared to your child's needs but if it makes you feel better about yourself, more rested and invigorated, it is well worth doing. For some it might be a swim or a walk, for others the chance to read a book in peace or to go shopping and be able to try clothes on. Find time to do whatever you want by sending your child to respite care or friends. If you have a break, you will return to your child feeling refreshed, you will feel better about yourself and be able to give more to your child.

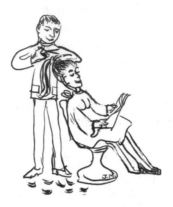

Find time to do what you want

- If you feel overloaded by appointments and commitments, remember **it is okay to say 'no' to professionals**. Sometimes if your child has special needs and associated medical problems you can feel that you are looking after a medical 'case' rather than caring for your own child. Professionals need to know what your daily life and responsibilities are and adjust their expectations accordingly. If you feel overwhelmed, ask which is the most important issue and deal with that alone. Alternatively, take a break, have time just to enjoy your child and then come back to all the playgroups and therapies when you are ready.

- **Don't feel guilty about saying 'no' to your child** if you can't or don't want to do something he wants to do. You have as much right as he has to choose activities and you also have a view of your day and domestic responsibilities which your child cannot have. If your child wants to paint and it is going to make a terrible mess which you don't want to or haven't time to clear up, say 'no'. Children have to learn that their desires cannot be met in full all the time because they have to consider the needs and wishes of others. It only becomes a problem if you do it too often. You also have to remember that they then have a right to say 'no' to you!

- **If you cannot cope, don't be afraid to admit it** and get help from your GP or health visitor.

How much parents can do

Parents are in a unique position with regard to their child. They are usually with him the most and know him best. They are the most important people in his life. By stimulating him, by providing security and support, by seeking help for him, by following his progress and moving him on and above all by loving him, they help their child develop.

Parents have a role in helping their child's development but they are not working to a syllabus which has to be completed within a set time limit. Their role is wider than that of a teacher. They provide a base of unconditional love. Whatever children achieve or do not achieve parents will still love and care for them. Parents can simply enjoy being with their child, doing something or nothing, introducing him to new experiences or revisiting old and favourite ones. They provide a secure environment where a child can be confident and happy, not one where he is constantly being tested and stretched.

The phrase **'good enough mother/father'** is worth remembering (Winnicott 1971, p.10). Parents want to do everything possible to help their child and it is very easy for them to feel that they are not doing 'enough' and that they are not the perfect parent. But such feelings do not help anyone – the child or the parent. A 'good enough mother/father' is what parents are and all they have to be.

> All the specialists bombard you with leaflets and things to do and you feel as if you should be doing everything all at once and that you are never doing enough. Also there seems little reward especially when your child is unresponsive. I read somewhere: **Whatever you do Is enough**.

Parents should have confidence in their skills and abilities as parents and have the courage to rely on their intuitive understanding of their child's needs and desires. Finding out that a child has special needs can knock a parent's confidence, particularly if the diagnosis comes as a total surprise. When a child is the subject of a stream of therapists and consultants the idea that parenting is a natural and innate skill can seem implausible. If it takes a team of professional experts to help a child learn to sit up and eat his food, what role does an amateur parent have? Parents play a vital role and the best care a child can receive is when parents and professionals work together with a true understanding of a child's needs. Therapists may suggest an approach but a parent will probably have an instinctive view of whether it is likely to work or not or how it should be modified to suit their particular child. Parents who trust their instincts and play with their child in a way that feels right for them and their child are usually right. Because parents know their child so well, they will also know when things aren't right and seek help.

A child does not exist in isolation – he is always part of a relationship, with his mother, his father and his siblings. Relationships are about two people not just one. So when looking at a child's needs, those of the parents and other siblings need to be considered too. A child who is cared for tirelessly by a mother who ignores her own needs and those of the rest of the family is not in a healthy relationship. On the other hand, a mother who is gaining something from her child and from time away from her child is happier and more confident, and of course ultimately gives more to the child. When you think about your child's needs you must remember your own needs too.

Parents who are motivated, interested and tenacious can sometimes do amazing things for their child with special needs. However, before selflessly dedicating their lives to their child they should look carefully at the wider issues and their other responsibilities:

PERSONAL NEEDS
Many new parents feel that a continuous round of feeding, changing, bathing and cuddling has swallowed up all their time and opportunities to pursue former interests. Gradually the chance to do aerobics or watch football matches returns as life becomes a bit easier. But having a child with special needs can make parents feel particularly guilty about taking time away from their child to do something which they find satisfying but which seems in the context to be rather frivolous. Such parents inevitably have less time for themselves but it is important that they do make time to do something for their own personal enjoyment and self-esteem.

RELATIONSHIPS WITH FAMILY AND FRIENDS
Parents need to make time to ensure that their relationships with their partner, other children and other family members can still flourish. This is discussed further in the rest of the chapter.

Relationship with your partner

Having a baby puts many relationships under strain as each person adjusts to his or her new role and the changed relationship. In particular, fathers can feel excluded by the close emotional and physical bond between mother and baby. In addition, the mother may feel that she has the whole burden of looking after the child while the father feels that he is doing his bit bringing in his salary. If he is unable to attend appointments and to see his child with other children of a similar age he may also have more difficulty accepting his child has special needs at all. Finding out you have a child with special needs may mean unhappiness and additional stress for you and for your partner. The experience will throw a sharp spotlight on all aspects of a relationship and may open up areas of weakness or disagreement which in normal circumstances might have gone undetected.

Strategies

- **Listen to each other** and respect each other's feelings and views. The mother, if she is the main carer, can sometimes feel that she knows her child best but the father has a unique position and a valid viewpoint and should not be ignored.

- **Make sure you both go to important appointments** with medical and educational professionals and are both fully aware of your child's condition and developmental progress and can then discuss issues jointly as they arise.

- **Don't make assumptions** about your partner. Find out what your partner thinks about important issues, don't just assume that you know how he or she feels.

- Remember that **different people come to terms with situations in different ways**. Your partner may not be showing grief in the same way as you but it does not mean that he feels it any less keenly.

- **Don't fall into the trap of making your views more extreme than they really are** in order to contradict your partner's view. Sometimes one partner can paint a very dire picture of the situation, making the other take a more upbeat view than he or she really feels and irritating the first into even more extreme views. You can find your views and selves polarized and it can feel as if one partner is refusing to accept there is a problem. If you were being honest you would probably accept that neither is saying what he or she really thinks and that your views are closer than they appear. This problem can be exacerbated by the fact that parents often have very little information to go on about their child's condition. Seek out more information so that you can both come to a better understanding.

- **Help each other out**. Try to ensure that family responsibilities have been divided reasonably and that each partner is doing their fair share. Each couple will work things out differently according to preferences and situation. If you really cannot help in one area make sure you take the burden in other areas.

I look after the children full-time and John goes to work full-time. I don't mind at all because I know when he comes home at 6pm he takes over completely and gives them baths and puts them to bed. Meanwhile I clear up and cook our supper. Once supper is over John washes up and clears away and my evening starts. We have an ironing lady so that I don't feel I have piles of ironing hanging over me every evening and we do the absolute minimum of cleaning. It seems to work.

- **Be prepared to rethink your lifestyle radically**. People often have preconceptions about how they are going to cope when they have children, whether the mother will go back to work, whether they can still go trekking round the Himalayas and how they will divide up household chores. Things rarely turn out as they think they will. When a child has special needs, things are usually more difficult and you have to be prepared to look at your situation objectively, decide on priorities and take appropriate action. Working long hours away from home with a long commute might put too much of a strain on the main carer and the working partner may have to seek work which allows him or her to spend more time at home.

- **Find time to be together without the children**. Get a baby-sitter and go out somewhere, even if it is just to the local pub for a chat for an hour or so. Talk about your views on your child's situation and what it means for your partner and for you. Also make sure you talk about things other than your child to give you a chance to rebalance your relationship.

Your other children

If you have other children too you will find that they often have very strong feelings of love, concern and responsibility for their disabled brother or sister.

> On holiday one day, Daniel (aged 8) told us how he planned to go mountain biking when he was grown up, but he was worried because it would mean there was no one at home to look after his disabled brother. It shocked us because we had never ever suggested to him that he would be responsible for his brother.

Children may take huge pleasure in their disabled brother's achievements and successes but as in all sibling relationships there can be intense jealousies compounded by the inevitable stresses and limitations of living with a disabled child. Inevitably a child with special needs will require more attention, special equipment and hospital visits and generate more stress, but a way has to be found of showing the other children that they are loved and valued and that their own needs are recognized. From the age of about seven, children also start noticing that their brother or sister is 'different'. Much may depend on the individual situation, the disability and the age of the children but it is very dangerous to get so wrapped up in the problems of one child that problems with others go unrecognized. The resentment that some siblings feel for the way their parents devoted all their time and energy to their disabled brother or sister and not to them can last for years, sometimes for ever. The impact of being a sibling of a disabled child (such as the caring responsibilities, lack of attention, low self-esteem, bullying) is being increasingly recognized through new initiatives. For more information contact Sibs (see Chapter 11) or visit www.youngcarer.com or www.youngcarers.net.

When dividing up parental attention and deciding on family priorities it is impossible to get the balance right all the time, but some of the following strategies may be helpful:

Strategies

- **Talk to your other children** about their feelings, acknowledge the difficulties, whilst remaining positive about their disabled brother. Talk about his condition or disability, make it clear that it is not their fault, they are not responsible and are not expected to care for him when grown up.

- **Do not have unrealistic expectations** of your other children. Unconsciously parents can sometimes impose extremely high standards of behaviour and achievement on their other children, who can sometimes also feel that they must 'make up' for their brother's disability. Remember that they are just children and need to be able to explore and experiment.

- **Make sure your other children have the opportunity, at least occasionally, to do activities** that they enjoy but which are difficult or impossible with their disabled brother around. Use respite care, divide up as a family or ask friends or relatives to help so that you can have a game of tennis or go and watch a film for a change.

- I think it is worth **challenging the perception that they are ignored** and sidelined by pointing out all the things you do for them, which they may not appreciate or be aware of. It is also useful sometimes to show the positive aspects of having a disabled brother – jumping the queue at theme parks or special trips out.

- **Ensure that your other children have a space** where they can get away from their brother and where their possessions are safe by putting a lock on the bedroom door or by creating a personal space.

- Give your children the opportunity to **meet other siblings** in a similar situation. It is helpful for them to realize they are not alone.

- If your disabled child is aggressive to his siblings or behaves embarrassingly or inappropriately in public, which some siblings find very difficult to cope with as they do not like being in the spotlight, try to **tackle it through behaviour management techniques** (see Chapter 9).

- **Find activities which you can all enjoy together**, whether it is swimming, watching a video as a family or going to the park.

Relationship with family and friends

Parents usually look to their own family and friends to give them support when they find out that they have a child with special needs. Inevitably some people will be more sensitive and aware and give better support than others.

Families

Coming from a different generation, grandparents have grown up when attitudes to children with special needs were quite different. The fact that forty years ago children with special needs were largely considered uneducable shows how far we have come. Unless they already have direct experience of children with special needs, grandparents may well need to change their own attitudes and face the reactions of their contemporaries. They too will have to come to terms with their own sadness about the news of their grandchild and their disappointed dreams. Parents can often feel that rather than getting any support from their own parents they are having to prop them up as well.

Some parents find that their families can focus exclusively on the 'problem' and forget that there is a child in there too. This is particularly true when special needs are identified at birth. Parents still want time to celebrate and enjoy the birth of a new and wonderful baby and do not want to be forever reminded of the problems ahead.

On the other hand, some grandparents may refuse to accept there is a problem, never allude to it and dismiss your efforts to get help. Tell them that they are not being helpful to you or your child.

I have always found the best policy is to be entirely open about Josh's problems because I feel if you don't recognize the problem, you don't appreciate the achievements.

Relationships with grandparents vary enormously but if you have good relationships then it is worth keeping the grandparents informed and getting them involved. Grandparents are in a unique position of trust, love and involvement and so can be a great source of help. With a different lifestyle, they can often access different information and advice. On the other hand, as they may have a lot more time than you, they can sometimes add to your stress with such questions as 'Have you contacted so and so yet?' or 'Have you read that article yet?'

Friends

People generally are not very good at talking to those in highly charged emotional situations. They often find it so difficult to say something appropriate that they end up saying nothing – which can be more hurtful because most people facing grief or loss prefer to talk about it.

> I have very strong memories of a dinner party with friends from my ante-natal group held two weeks after Aisha's first diagnosis. We talked about all the children but Elizabeth was carefully ignored. I remember feeling as if I did not really exist. My whole being was consumed by this concern and love for my daughter and this devastating news and yet I wasn't allowed to talk about it. Later I realized that it was up to me to talk about it. Now if I set the tone by talking about my child, saying what is happening and what she is doing, my friends respond really well.

If you don't talk about your child, your friends will assume you don't want to and keep quiet themselves. Good friends are an enormous source of strength and support so try to get the relationship to work.

How to cope with public reactions

While researching this book, it became clear that many parents had experienced some awful reactions from people because of the appearance or behaviour of their child.

Everyone responds to such reactions differently according to circumstances, the child involved, their own personality and how they feel on any given day. There is no right response. Sometimes you feel brave and strong and are able to challenge people's assumptions and rudeness; other times you just move on and away as quickly as you can, often wishing afterwards that you could have thought of a witty put-down.

Alternatively, you can meet people who think they are being helpful by being terribly positive or over-sympathetic. They make comments like

'Oh well, he looks alright to me', 'Oh, but my child does that as well' or 'Oh, how terrible for you'.

Strategies

- Remember **your primary duty is to your child** and not to educate other people in equal opportunities and common humanity. Keep your child safe and keep doing what you need to do in order to help your child in the long term. If other people cannot handle this then it is their problem and not yours.

- **If someone makes an adverse comment, you could try saying something** like 'I'm sorry you find Amy's behaviour distressing but she does have cerebral palsy/ autism/ a heart condition' and then move away quickly.

If Mohammed starts misbehaving and I detect hostility, I use sign language to him in a very exaggerated way, so that people can pick up on the fact that he has special needs. They then either back off immediately or very occasionally ask if he is deaf or talk about signing.

- It is important to lead as 'normal' a life as possible for your own sake and for that of all your children. You must go out, go shopping, go to the park and visit people. However, it is sensible to know your own limits and those of your child. **There is no point making yourself miserable to prove a point.** Some shops are geared up for children and have helpful and understanding staff; try to avoid ones which aren't. Some days you may feel up to going out and about with your child, other days you may be feeling fragile and prefer to stay at home. Be realistic. When you have children, certain activities become difficult or impossible. Just make sure you do have time through respite care or family help to do things that are important to you.

- **Be careful not to jump to conclusions about people's attitudes** towards you and your child. It is very easy when you are out with your child who is drawing attention to himself to think that people are condemning you as an ineffective parent and your child as badly behaved. Sometimes you know because they say as much but other times they may merely be looking at you out of curiosity and feeling sympathy and support.

I live in a small village where I frequently go shopping with my two children. In the grocer's Tom has an obsession with the dog food, the Frosties and cucumbers, in the Post Office with the batteries and in the newsagent with the chilled drinks cabinet. One day I had a miserable time doing battle in each of these shops trying to stop Tom pulling things off the shelf and wrecking everything. I felt the shopkeepers and customers were staring at me disapprovingly and at Tom in horror. I seriously wondered if it was feasible to go shopping again with him. The next day I went in on my own and Karen in the newsagent amazed me by asking me where I found the energy to deal with Tom and commenting on how much he had improved. She noticed that he used signs (Makaton) and asked to be taught how to say 'hello' to him. Rather than being disapproving she had actually been really supportive and I had completely mis-judged her and probably many others.

When I see other parents having 'problems' with their child's behav-iour, I try to 'look supportive' but they probably interpret my look as one of a smug and judgemental mother. It is very difficult to show solidarity and support without appearing nosy and interfering.

Diagnosis

When parents first find out that their child has special needs they rarely get an immediate and specific diagnosis of, say, dyspraxia or cerebral palsy but are more likely to receive a label of global developmental delay, communication delay or something else equally vague and non-specific. It may take months if not years to get a full diagnosis and many never receive one at all.

A diagnosis can seem vitally important. Parents hope that it will provide the 'answer' to their child's problems – a blueprint for how to treat the child and a vision of what the future holds. Equally, parents are often concerned that they are responsible in some way for their child's condition and therefore want to know the 'cause' to eradicate the sus-picion of guilt. They may also need to know if there are any genetic implications which may affect their decision whether or not to have

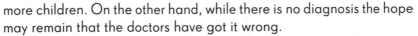

more children. On the other hand, while there is no diagnosis the hope may remain that the doctors have got it wrong.

A diagnosis is useful in many ways. After the initial shock, parents can start to come to terms with their child's condition and his situation. It can be a low point, but once they know the worst, they can move on, start looking forward and be positive. It can make things easier with other people. If you say your child has 'special needs' with no diagnosis, you may be regarded as a neurotic parent by some people or as a parent who is making excuses for his or her child's poor performance or behaviour.

> In our case saying our son is autistic seemed a lot more acceptable as an excuse for extraordinary behaviour than saying he has special needs.

As parents, you can start to access organizations and help groups relevant to your child's special needs. These can provide extremely useful support, information and ideas and access to other parents in similar situations.

There is a perception that having a diagnosis helps with the provision of services by health and education, but this ought not to be the case since children should be considered on the basis of their needs not by their label.

However, if you do have a diagnosis, remember the points below. Equally, if you don't have a diagnosis consider these before expending huge amounts of money and energy on seeking one.

A child with special needs is a unique individual and should always be considered in this way. You should always think about the child and not the label. The kind of support and education he requires will be determined by his needs alone. A diagnosis can push children down a particular route for care or education which may not be appropriate. Just because children with Down's Syndrome generally follow a certain developmental pattern it does not follow that every child with Down's Syndrome will. The usual approach may not be appropriate for your child.

Similarly most 'labels' cover such a huge spectrum of abilities that they don't actually give you any real clue as to what the future holds, let alone a blueprint. Only think of the range of abilities within the spectrum of autism, Down's Syndrome or cerebral palsy. A diagnosis may give you access to more information but parents still have to search for help, labour over decisions and wait and see how things unfold.

I found out Christopher had special needs when he was one and then when he was three, at a routine meeting with his consultant, we were given a working diagnosis of autism. I remember thinking with relief 'Oh so that's what you call Christopher'. Get the label to fit the child, do not force the child to fit the label.

Some parents get hung up on searching for a diagnosis. A child won't be any different just because he has a convenient label. In the end, it is just a label and energies are probably better spent on other activities.

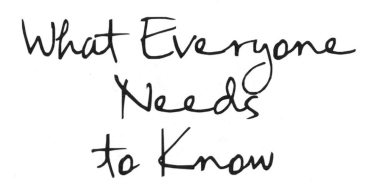

CHAPTER 2

What Everyone Needs to Know

This chapter looks at simple changes you can make in our approach and home environment which can be of benefit to your children whatever their special needs. It outlines different strategies which will give you the best chance of success in play and everyday life. It also offers some suggestions of activities to help with issues which require special attention such as motivation and the need for repetition.

Creating the right environment for play

All children are easily distracted by activities and objects around them. In addition, if they have little interest in what they are doing, have physical problems which make concentrating difficult or have particular problems with attention, they may be particularly flitty. It is therefore important to create a home environment which is as conducive as possible to learning. If your child has particular sensitivities which may need to be taken into consideration it is worth reading the section on sensory integration on pp.154–155. Consider the following aspects of the environment:

Timing

Find a time to play with your child when she is alert and happy, not hungry or tired, and when you have time, energy and enthusiasm to devote to her. Choose a time when you are unlikely to be disturbed and when you are not distracted by other tasks. You are then more likely to get a positive response.

Noise

Having a television, radio or music on, while doing other things, makes it more difficult to concentrate. If you are trying to play constructively with your child, it is a good idea to turn everything off and let her concentrate. If she has a hearing loss or a language problem this is doubly important because she will need to concentrate on what you are saying and will find it very difficult if noise from elsewhere is competing.

Distractions

When you play with your child clear the table or floor space of clutter and unnecessary toys. Keep out only the toy you are playing with. As you finish with toys do not leave them lying around but put them away, out of sight in a box or bag. This way your child will not be distracted by the next or previous activity and will be more likely to stay on track.

Some children can be easily distracted

Clear the table of any unnecessary toys

If you have a child who is very easily distracted and who fiddles with everything, keep your house as free of clutter as you can. Some children can be very easily distracted by things such as toys, ornaments and clutter and you may have to make quite drastic changes to aid concentration. Some children need a low-arousal environment with minimal furnishings and subdued colours.

Working at the dining table or on a low table may help because it will be more difficult for your child to see other distractions and to run away.

To minimize distractions, you could consider creating a 'work bay' for your child in your house like ones often used in special schools. In these schools children often work at a table which is placed in a bay with high plain walls on three sides so they cannot see out and are therefore encouraged to concentrate on the activities given to them. Children learn the idea of working from left to right because tasks are placed on their left, they then work on them and move them to the right once completed. This may seem a very drastic measure for the home but you can use the idea of placing a table in a quiet corner against plain walls. Some children respond well to having a specific place for 'working'. The idea of a 'work bay' is particularly used in TEACCH, which is a programme devised in the USA for children with autism and communication disorders (see Chapter 11, Resources).

Seating

Many children will play and concentrate very happily while sitting on the floor or at a conventional table. However, if your child has a physical disability of any kind then her position and seating should be considered.

A child who is poorly positioned so that she feels uncomfortable, insecure or unsupported will be concentrating on stabilizing herself rather than doing any other activity you give her. If she is using her hands to prop herself up, she will not be able to use them to play. A child, on the other hand, who is comfortable and properly supported will be in a good position to play and free to concentrate. Equally a child who is extremely fidgety will benefit from proper seating because she will be encouraged to sit still and because she will find it more difficult to escape and evade you.

Correct sitting positions

There are all sorts of seating options you could think about including a specialist chair, a low table and chair, a high chair or a chair at the dining table. Consider your child's particular circumstances and discuss any requirements with your occupational therapist.

On the other hand, if balance is not a problem, it is often good to experiment with different seating positions because they can help with physical skills. Playing on the floor, at a table or when kneeling at a coffee table requires different postures and develops different muscles.

Lighting

Good bright lighting is important for everyone and for a child with a visual impairment clear bright light is vital to allow her to use and develop the sight that she has. On the other hand, a child with an over-sensitivity to bright lights might need low, subtle lighting.

Your position when playing with your child

Always sit directly opposite your child when playing with her and talking to her. It will then be easy for her to make eye contact with you, to see your face, mouth, eyes and expression and to see what you are doing and to copy it. If you sit next to her, you will make it more difficult for her to see what you are doing since she will only get a sideways view and will not be able to see your face very easily. The same advice holds for other non-play situations, for instance if you are trying to encourage your child to feed herself, turn her high chair to face you directly rather than have her sit alongside you. Avoid standing or sitting in front of a window with your face in darkness.

Making activities achievable

Devise activities which your child has a good chance of completing successfully. The following sections show ways of doing this.

Break skills down into small steps

You can make things easier for your child by breaking new skills down into smaller and more manageable steps. Rather than trying to teach a new skill in one go, aim to get there gradually. For example, if you want to get your child to feed herself with a spoon, start by loading a spoon with food, then get her to lift the spoon to her mouth, probably by placing your hand over hers and taking it to her mouth. Then when she can do that, get her to put the spoon back in the bowl and finally to scoop the food onto the spoon.

Similarly, if you are potty training your child start by concentrating on getting her to wee or poo in the potty and do the other bits like undressing, bottom wiping, dressing and handwashing for her. As she becomes ready you can get her to take on more of the process. She might then become able to pull her trousers or tights down, later pull them up again and wash her hands until finally she is able to do the whole routine with guidance and ultimately independently.

Start by making things easy

Introduce any new skill by using toys which are easy for your child to use and understand. Then as she becomes more competent gradually make the games more challenging for her. So don't get out your 2000-piece jigsaw puzzle when you want to play with puzzles but find one with two or three pieces. Find chunky blocks to thread with a thick and firm cord before moving on to cotton reels and beads using a flimsy cord. If you are concentrating on feeding with a spoon, start with food like yoghurt which sticks to the spoon and then progress slowly to more difficult consistencies like pasta or thin soups.

Start with objects which fit comfortably into your child's hand and which she can manipulate easily. Very large objects can be as difficult to handle as very tiny ones.

Forward and backward chaining

There are also two useful techniques called forward and backward chaining. Think of an activity as a chain or sequence of tiny actions. Forward chaining is when you get a child to perform the first action in the sequence which you then complete, and backward chaining is when you get a child to perform the last action in the sequence which you have started. You then gradually increase the amount your child has to do as she becomes more competent until she is doing the whole thing.

For instance, if you want your child to wash her face you might use forward chaining. Get her to start by putting her hands in a basin of water, then finish the action yourself. As she becomes more competent get her to bring her hands to her face, then wash it and later still dry it. Alternatively, if you want your child to build a tower, use forward chaining by getting her to place the first brick on the floor and then place the bricks on top yourself. Later get her to place two bricks, one on top of the other and then complete the tower yourself. Gradually get her to build more of the tower with you doing the top fiddly bricks until she is able to do them all.

Backward chaining: put the last piece in the jigsaw

If you want your child to do a jigsaw puzzle use backward chaining. Complete the puzzle except for the very last piece. Then get your child to put in the last piece so she gets all the excitement of completing the picture and finishing the puzzle. Then as she improves, get her to insert more pieces. Choose the chaining method which enables her to do the easy and rewarding part and then build on her success.

Be aware of where your child is developmentally

Follow your child's developmental progress and see what sort of skills she should be working towards. If you give your child something to do which is way beyond her she will have little chance of success, quickly lose interest and become frustrated and angry.

Motivation

Children with special needs often do not have a great urge to explore and experiment with toys. They may need to be given the motivation to learn.

Use your child's interests

You can use your understanding of what interests and excites your child to provide motivation.

Most skills can be learned in a variety of situations and the key to success is often picking the right way of introducing a new idea or skill. Putting objects in a box is a very important skill but it is deeply unexciting. You can make it more interesting by using objects which make a good noise as they hit the container or by holding the box and making the objects jump out after they have gone in. If your child finds it amusing she is much more likely to be motivated to carry on playing.

Children often have a particular activity which they enjoy and which you can use in a variety of ways to teach different skills. Later, once the skill is reasonably established, it can be more easily extended to other activities which are perhaps less interesting. For example, if your child likes games where things move and happen, you could try playing with a marble run which has different coloured pieces. These can be put together and used in a number of ways:

- practice at putting marbles in the run (since marbles are quite small this is good for children's fine motor skills)

- practice at building and fitting things together (one child had no interest in Duplo and other building materials but the marble run element provided the motivation)

- turn-taking (take turns at putting the marbles in or building the run)

- practice at colours – matching ('give me a piece like this'), colour selecting ('give me a blue one') and colour naming ('what colour is this?')

- number practice ('give me one piece', 'give me two pieces')

- language (building 'up', marbles going 'in', marbles coming 'out').

How to praise and encourage

Children with special needs often need a lot of exaggerated praise and encouragement because they may not readily pick up and respond to adult pleasure and approval.

Children need exaggerated praise and encouragement

Praise has to be exaggerated and over the top. When a child does something particularly good for the first time, give lots of praise (spoken and signed) with big smiles, laughter and clapping to reinforce what you are saying. It can then be toned down as the skill becomes more commonplace.

> When Madeleine first walked from one side of the room to the other the whole family came to admire and praise her to ensure that she realized she had done something good, but six months on it is no longer noteworthy.

Children do not necessarily know what they have done which is so good, so you must refer to it when you are praising them. 'Good boy' or 'Good girl' is too abstract. You should say 'Good waving', 'Nice talking', 'Good pooing in the potty' or 'Good sitting still'. Then your child knows which action is the one that has earned the praise. It may sound a bit silly but it is the best way to reinforce their good behaviour.

Try to be positive and encouraging with your child. Get yourself in a mind-set where you look at her attempts in a positive rather than a negative way and concentrate on successes while ignoring failures. If your child tries to put her trousers on and gets both legs in one hole you can say 'Well done for trying to put your trousers on. Look this leg goes in this hole' or you can say 'No, you're doing it all wrong, you've got both legs in the same hole'. One approach is positive and encouraging, the other is demotivating. Children respond much better to the carrot than the stick.

Always give your child the benefit of the doubt if you think she may be attempting a new skill. It can be difficult to be certain that she is attempting something new – it can be so fleeting that it seems just to be a coincidence or a fluke. However, you should always assume that it is deliberate and conscious and therefore reward, praise and encourage your child. If it does turn out to be mere coincidence you haven't lost anything. There is nothing worse than realizing afterwards that you have been ignoring your child's best efforts to practise some new skill.

Rewards

If your child does not find your praise and encouragement sufficiently motivating, you can of course use tangible rewards. Obvious ones are drinks, food and cuddles. Other rewards could be games or activities depending on your child's interests: perhaps a chance to read a book or play with a favourite toy or game.

> Rebecca has always liked bubbles and will do most things for the chance to play with them. When beginning potty training, we found them useful as a reward for getting her to sit on the potty. Once there we hoped she would perform so that we could then praise her 'efforts'. It worked and once she had got the idea we abandoned the bubbles quite easily and just kept up the praise.

To use rewards effectively keep them small, immediate and under your control. Use them slightly randomly so that your child sometimes gets one for free and sometimes gets none. This will prevent her getting totally fixated on the reward because you do want her to learn to enjoy the task for its own sake. For example, blow a few bubbles when your child does what you want, occasionally do not blow any and sometimes blow some for free. You could try a packet of crisps broken into small pieces, hold them behind your back and give them out as and when they are needed. If you give the child the whole packet once she has done something for you, you have lost an opportunity to gain a lot more co-operation. Young children need to see an immediate connection between their behaviour and the reward. They will not understand the promise of a trip to the swings the next day until they are quite 'old'.

With rewards it is worth remembering that:

- you eventually want praise and success at an activity to be enough motivation by themselves and the rewards to be less crucial, otherwise you will be forever bargaining with your child

- you have to be even-handed in giving out rewards – if you have other children you may not feel it is always appropriate to be rewarding one child and not the others

- if you use sweets and biscuits as a reward, remember your child's teeth and health.

Rotating and varying toys

Children (and adults) get bored with toys that are around all the time. They may have a toy box full of toys but they cannot find anything to play with. Keep a good half of your toys in the loft or in cupboards and change them round every few months. Keep out the things your child is playing with, making sure you have a variety of toys (for example, not all cars or all posting tins), and put the rest away. When you rotate the toys your child will probably jump on the 'new' toys as if she had never seen them before. Don't worry that you will not have enough toys out. Like the clothes in your cupboard, children only ever seem to play with a relatively small percentage of the toys available.

You can borrow toys relatively cheaply from the toy libraries organized by the National Association of Toy and Leisure Libraries (see Chapter 11, p.257). Alternatively you could try exchanging toys with friends.

General issues for children with special needs

There are a number of difficulties that children with special needs face which you may need to address in your approach.

Give your child longer to respond than you think she needs

It seems we are programmed as parents to give our children a certain amount of time to respond to us by smiling, talking or playing. When you see mothers cooing to their babies they give them a limited time to coo back before moving on to another activity. There is a remarkable conformity in the time parents allow for a response (Cunningham et al. 1981; Jones 1977). However, special needs children can take a lot longer to respond, so parents should consciously allow them longer before turning away. For example, children with cerebral palsy often need a long time to 'process' requests and organize movements like eye pointing or touching objects. When you are playing with your child and want a smile, a noise or a word and have had enough of waiting for a response, count to ten and wait again. Give your child plenty of time. Be patient.

Give your child plenty of time to respond

Repetition and perseverance

You will probably find yourself repeating and repeating and repeating words, actions or gestures in order that eventually your child will understand and respond. There is no substitute for repetition even though you may feel as if you are banging your head against a brick wall.

> For years with Jack we repeated simple words – mummy, daddy, bath-time, drink etc. – at appropriate moments, practised putting in and on, played peek-a-boo with a cloth, all with absolutely no response. Then eventually we did get a response – a passive understanding and then an active involvement and it was all worthwhile.

> Looking back, the things we did with mind-numbing repetitiveness are beginning to pay off now. Right from the start we would talk to Natasha at every opportunity. 'Show me your foot. Yes there's your foot.' I would point. Everyday. Now Natasha lifts her foot right up to her head without prompting and points to my foot, her shoe, my shoe and everybody else's shoes.

Lack of response

One of the hardest things to cope with as a parent is the lack of response that children with special needs often display. It is very draining to be constantly giving a child love, attention, time and care and feel that she is giving nothing back. There is little you can do except persevere and love your child. You will be rewarded even if it is only in a small way.

See Chapter 8, pp.193–194 for ideas on how to get a response from your child and Chapter 1, p.19, on strategies for coping with the stresses and strains of having a child with special needs.

Using visual and other sensory supports

Most children will benefit from a multi-sensory approach to communication and learning. It is clearly vital for those with a sensory impairment but is equally beneficial for those with poor communication skills and indeed it will help all children. We tend to use predominantly verbal information and instructions and children with auditory processing problems find it difficult to take in, understand and then respond to the information given.

You may find that certain approaches work better for you personally depending on how you prefer to get your information. If you try to remember directions, you may prefer to draw a map, act them out with your hands or repeat them to yourself. In the same way children often have a preference and are described accordingly as visual, kinaesthetic (by movement) or aural (by listening) learners. There is now a great awareness of different 'learning styles' by teachers and schools. Most of us may have a bias towards one style but use different strategies depending on the circumstances.

Many children with special needs respond particularly well to the use of visual supports such as actual objects, pictures or photographs, so try to incorporate these into your daily life to help their understanding. You might show a sponge when talking about bath-time, or a shopping bag when going to the supermarket. Digital cameras or mobile phones are a brilliant way of enabling you to take photos of actual places, people and things such as your child's cup, playgroup or granny. So when you talk you can give a visual prompt by showing a photograph. If you are 'going to playgroup' show a photo of the particular playgroup or if you want her to 'get her shoes' show a picture of shoes. If your child has a choice between a drink of milk or juice, you could show the cartons or photographs to enable her to understand the question and make a decision. You could try labelling relevant objects around the house, such as the child's chair or potty, and then use corresponding labels when talking about them. As well as saying the words you can also use the Makaton or Signalong sign for the word to add further reinforcement (see pp.103–104 for more details of signing systems).

Remember also the phrase 'Hear, see, do'. Rather than just talk about an object, try to engage the other senses at the same time as appropriate. So if you are talking about different fruits, look at them, feel and touch them, smell them, shake them and taste them too. Your child is much more likely to understand you than if you just point out a picture in a book. For a child who picks things up much better kinaesthetically (i.e. by movement) try guiding her hands with your hands so that they are actually doing the action (hand-over-hand method) rather than just telling or showing her what to do.

Routines and predictability

Children thrive on routines and structure in their lives because they enable them to understand what is going on around them and to recognize and eventually predict situations, creating a feeling of understanding and security and allaying some of their anxieties.

If your child has a communication problem or a sensory impairment, she may find it difficult to pick up on what is going on and make sense of it. It is therefore even more important that you stick to the same basic routine each day. Keep the environment the same; for example, don't keep changing the furniture around if your child has a visual impairment. Make sure that you are consistent in your response to your child's behaviour, particularly bad behaviour. Children have to go out into the world where so much is unknown and try to make sense of it all. It is a lot easier if they have learnt that their own home environment is governed by a kind of timetable (e.g. getting up and going to bed at certain times, having regular meals) and by social manners (e.g. sitting down to eat and drink). However, routine does not mean rigidity, for instance bed-time does not necessarily have to be on the dot of 7.00 but it should be between 6.30 and 7.30, say, and not between 7.00 and 10.00. Also some children get fixated on routines and so need some variation within the routine to prevent fixations from occurring.

VISUAL TIMETABLES

Children who find it difficult to cope with an open-ended situation and like structure in their lives may find it helpful to have timetables with pictures so that they can see how their day is organized and what they are going to do next.

Visual timetables are developed in the TEACCH programme (see Chapter 11, Resources). This is a system used with children with autism and communication disorders. It is detailed and complex but the following shows how it can be used in a simplified way in the home.

The timetable might cover a whole day with a morning activity, lunch, afternoon activity, tea and bed, or it might cover a few hours only. It should be organized according to the needs of the child.

Put Velcro on a board or strip of card or wood to which you can then attach pictures or objects. The timetable should run from left to right or from top to bottom.

Use objects, photographs, pictures, symbols or words to depict each activity on the timetable.

Visual timetable

Below is a list of the different formats you can use from the simplest to the most sophisticated. Choose the form most appropriate to your child's level of understanding.

- Use actual objects to indicate an activity. For example, breakfast could be a spoon, swimming could be an arm band, lunch could be a banana and a shopping trip could be a carrier bag.

- Use clear photographs of actual objects or of your child doing a specific activity. Playgroup could be a photograph of your child at playgroup, a trip to the supermarket could be a photograph of your child in her supermarket trolley, a visit from Granny could be a picture of Granny in your home.

- Use simple line drawings of the activity. Draw a picture of a bowl of Frosties, horse riding or the car.

- Use symbols to show the activities. Makaton publish a range of symbols which are clear, stylized, line drawings (see p.256).

- Finally, use words just as anybody would do in a diary, such as 10.00 playgroup, 1.00 lunch.

If the timetable works for your child and you use it over a period of time, move your child on to the next level when she is ready. When you are making the transition from one stage to the next use both methods in conjunction for a period.

Although it may seem very complicated initially, most children in fact only have a limited number of activities and so you will only need to create a dozen or so pictures which you can then re-use as necessary. If something unexpected comes up, you can use an exclamation mark or an 'oops' symbol to indicate a change of plan.

Refer your child to her timetable throughout the day so that she can sense the structure and know what is about to happen. As each activity is completed remove the picture from the timetable.

The importance of generalizing skills

In order to say that a child has achieved a certain skill, she has to demonstrate that she can do it not just with familiar toys but with unknown objects, in all sorts of circumstances and for a variety of people. Professionals, in particular, always want evidence that a skill has been generalized in this way. For example, in order to say that a child can match pictures, she has to demonstrate this skill with any set of pictures – not just the ones she has been using at home. If she can do it with one set, she will certainly learn to do it with others, but she has to be given the opportunity.

Give your child lots of opportunities to use different materials in a variety of situations when playing so that she can learn to experiment and explore and expand her knowledge and understanding.

Don't get fixated on one skill

It is easy to get fixated on teaching your child one particular skill as if it will transform her life. It might be because of what people say to you – 'Is she sitting up yet?' or 'Is she walking?' – or because of your views of what is important. However, it is not usually helpful to have such a fixation. First, parents may then ignore all the other skills which are developing simultaneously and need to be recognized and encouraged. Second, it ignores the way children develop, which is as a whole. It is difficult to isolate one particular skill because skills develop in an inter-related and complicated way. For example, when a child puts an object in a box she needs the physical skill to grasp and release it and the intellectual skill to see the relationship between the sizes of the container and the object.

Equally, learning a new skill in one area will have a profound and beneficial effect on others where a connection is not necessarily immediately obvious. For example, an improvement in communication skills will mean a child has a greater understanding of social situations and how to behave. Learning to sit up will enable a child to handle toys better, explore them more, see what's going on around her and learn from that and, surprisingly, make a greater range of sounds.

Completing tasks

If you ask your child to do something and she does not want to or cannot do it then you should complete the task yourself saying, perhaps, 'Mummy put the piece in then'. The point is that you want your child to feel that it is important that she completes an activity or game. If she refuses to do something you have asked and you merely shrug and put it aside, she will form the impression that it does not matter whether or not she does it and will be less likely to co-operate in the future.

Stay in tune with your child

There is a danger in the way that we look at child development and, indeed, in the very nature of this book that parents become too focused on skill development, on the next stage and on comparisons with peers.

Follow your child in her play

As well as striving for progress as you see it, enjoy your child and follow her in her play, in her language and in her activities. Copy her. Go along with her. Enter her world and respect and learn what she is about. If you are doing something with your child and she does something unexpected do not necessarily correct her, go along with it and see what happens. Empathize with your child. See things from her point of view rather than always be trying to get her to conform to your own world and expectations.

Have high expectations

Have high expectations of what your child will achieve and don't impose barriers on her by saying she will never sit up or communicate, because she may do. Work towards her achieving all skills and fulfilling her potential. You will then give your child the opportunities, the respect and the environment she needs to develop. You may have to modify your expectations in the light of experience but it is best to aim for the top and fall short, knowing that you have done everything you can.

If you assume your child is capable of achieving very little, she will achieve very little because such an attitude is self-fulfilling. You can feel that you are being very hard forcing your child to do physical exercises or play games that she clearly does not enjoy but she will gradually start to enjoy them as they become familiar and easier. If in the end it means she becomes more independent, the benefit will be all hers.

Concentrate on small steps at a time. Give everything your best effort and demand that she does the same.

My sister and I had our babies close together. Her little boy was bringing back paintings from playgroup by the age of two. 'My Natasha will never do that' I thought negatively. 'She can't even sit up and she's nearly two.' Natasha is now three and a half. She not only sits up but is beginning to bear weight and her favourite subject at nursery is...painting! She also bakes cakes for me and is learning to play with sand. I am more patient now and certainly more optimistic.

CHAPTER 3

Cognitive Development

The theory

What are cognitive skills?

By exploring and experimenting with objects and their environment, children gain an understanding of how things work; they learn what the properties and capabilities of objects and materials are and they discover that they can affect and influence what happens around them. The cognitive skills which children acquire in pre-school years underlie later development in reading, writing and mathematics as well as conceptual and logical thought.

Chronological development

NEWBORN BABY

A newborn baby is primarily interested in people and faces. Given different things to look at a newborn or very young baby will choose to look at a face. A real face is the most interesting but babies are also attracted by pictures of faces, even if they are crudely drawn, imaginary or even grotesque.

COPYING

Babies copy adults from a very young age, for example by making faces or by sticking out their tongues. Copying is a crucial skill because it is by copying adults and other children that children learn to do new things and to say new words. It therefore underlies all development and is fundamental to learning cognitive skills.

EXPLORING OBJECTS

It is only after spending a long time observing faces and people that children become interested in exploring objects. Initially they take everything to their mouth because the mouth is the most sensitive part of the body and will therefore give them the most information about each object. Then they start to shake objects, to hit them against other surfaces, to examine them, feel them, drop and throw them. Using all their senses in this way children learn about the properties of each object – its feel and texture, whether it is hard or soft, heavy or light, the noise it makes, whether it tastes good, whether it changes shape or stays rigid and what it looks like from all angles.

OBJECT PERMANENCE

Children initially think that objects and people only exist when they can see them and that as soon as they have disappeared from sight they no longer exist. Consequently, a young child will cry when his mother leaves the room because he thinks she has vanished. He will not look for a toy that has rolled out of sight because, as far as he is concerned, it does not exist (Piaget 1953). (For a summary of Piaget's work on child development see Sime 1980.) Gaining an understanding that objects continue to exist even when they cannot be seen is a major development milestone, indicating that children have started to develop the ability to conceptualize. As a result of this particular understanding, they will start to look for things, accept absences and remember people, toys and actions instead of believing everything is new each time it appears. When children start dropping toys out of their pram or highchair and see their mothers returning them over and over again they start to get the idea of object permanence. They then watch to see where the toys go and to look for them. They learn to find partially covered toys and later wholly covered toys. They play peek-a-boo using a cloth because they know someone is still there even if hidden.

EXPLORING THE ENVIRONMENT

Once mobile, children want to explore their environment and find out about everything around them. They go through a phase of not being content with the box of toys in the middle of the carpet. They want to open and close all the doors, empty the cupboards and reach the precious ornaments on the top shelf. This is as important as exploring objects because through it children widen their understanding of their environment. They explore how things like doors work, they learn to examine the same things from different angles and they learn about natural phenomena like light, shade and echoes.

CAUSE AND EFFECT
Once children start playing with objects they learn that if they hit a rattle against a hard surface they will get a certain noise or that if they squeeze a certain ball they will hear a squeak. This is the start of learning about cause and effect. One of the easiest examples to think of is a child pressing a button on a pop-up toy and seeing that the animal jumps up. It takes a little time for him to realize that the animal popping up is a direct consequence of him pressing the button. Children learn all sorts of examples of cause and effect, for instance switching on lights, turning on the television and playing a keyboard.

Learning about cause and effect is a fundamental skill because it gives children the awareness that they can influence the objects and environment around them and that they live in a world which is, to an extent, controlled and controllable.

RELATIONAL PLAY
After mouthing, shaking and hitting objects, children go on to test how objects can be used in relation to others. For example they put a spoon in a cup, a brick in a box, a ball under a stool, or fill up and empty containers. They are beginning to make comparisons between objects, for example that 'this block is too big and will not go in' or 'that block has to be placed centrally otherwise it will fall off the top of the tower'. These kinds of comparisons about size, weight and placement are the start of mathematical thinking and the basis of conceptual thought.

BUILDING
As children play with more than one object and see how they can be combined, they start to build. Initially they build simple towers with large blocks and enjoy knocking them down. Then, as their fine motor skills improve, they learn to use smaller, fiddlier pieces and build taller towers as well as bridges and other constructions using bricks, Duplo, train tracks and other construction materials. They are learning about weight, shapes, three-dimensionial objects and size.

MATCHING, SELECTING AND NAMING
When learning a new concept children always learn in the order of match, select, name. First they first see that two objects are the same or

share similar qualities (matching), then they have a passive understanding (responding to being asked to select) and finally they are able to actively name the object.

Matching

Children first learn to match objects which are identical, e.g. this ball is the same as that ball and not that car. They start with actual objects like bricks or teddies, then they learn to match pictures of objects to the real thing and then to other pictures. Later they are able to match colours, then such concepts as big and little, long and short.

The ability to match, in other words to recognize similarities and differences, is a crucial skill for later mathematics and reading.

Selecting

Having learnt to match objects, children go on to select them. For example an adult asks a child to give him the picture of the train or the blue brick, where there is a choice of several pictures or objects. When selecting the child has to recognize and respond to the name but not to actively use it.

Naming

The final stage is for children to be able to name the object, picture or colour. So when shown a picture of a car the child says 'car'. This requires him to recall the name accurately.

SORTING AND GROUPING

Children learn to examine a set of objects and sort them into groups consisting of the same or similar things. For instance, when tidying up a child might sort his toys into a pile of Duplo and a pile of train track, or blue Lego and yellow Lego.

Later on they classify and group by a common factor, for instance putting all the cooking things together or all the bathroom things. This is a skill which we continue to use later in life to organize our possessions and environments, create order and aid thought processes and memory.

PRE-NUMERACY SKILLS

Children repeat numbers by rote from quite an early age but do not actually understand the concepts behind numbers for a long time. They have to learn that one means one thing, two means two things and so on (the so-called 'oneness of one'). They first learn 'one' and 'two', then 'lots/more' before learning further numbers.

Children also learn simple concepts which underlie mathematics such as big and small, long and short, heavy and light and the language of maths – capacity, weight, measure, big, bigger and biggest.

PRE-READING SKILLS

Children develop an understanding that writing conveys meaning, can be read and is the same every time it is read. They gain this by looking at books. They first look at picture books and are generally interested in the pictures. They then start to point to specific pictures and later to listen to simple stories which are read to them. After they have understood that pictures can convey meaning, they begin to realize that writing also has meaning, can be read and is understood. They learn that it is read the same every time. So when they look at familiar books which have often been read to them, they start to predict what is going to happen and fill in missing words from memory. Children sometimes get cross if you don't read it the same way each time.

The other component is an ability to match and remember the shapes of letters. Children first learn to match and recognize pictures and then move on to match symbols and finally letters. The first words they recognize are the most familiar ones such as their own names and those of family members which they see on labels, notes, cards, signs and in books.

PRE-WRITING SKILLS

Drawing and writing are complex skills which marry physical skill with cognitive understanding. To draw, a child not only needs the physical control and skill to make a mark, but he also needs to understand the relationship between the pen and the paper and to understand the idea that a mark can represent something.

Initially children just scribble randomly before becoming aware of the marks they are actually making. Then they consciously draw vertical then horizontal lines, dots then circles. They begin to control their movements and look at what they are doing and understand that they can control their marks. The usual sequence of marks is shown in the illustration below.

I — O + □ \ / △ X

The first marks a child makes

They learn that making marks has two purposes: to make shapes like a cross, triangle or square which can be made into pictures or alternatively to make letters such as A, B and C which can be used for communication. They start to copy simple symbols such as X, +, O, V, H and T and draw simple pictures of people and houses.

Parallel development

MEMORY

Babies can probably remember some things from birth because early on they remember the sound of their mother's voice and can recognize her face and smell. Children pick up on 'cues' which remind them of what is going to happen, for example they remember that the sound of a tap running indicates a bath. As they grow up their memory develops so that experiences and objects are remembered and do not seem new each time. They remember who people are, what things do and how to perform certain actions.

Once the idea of object permanence is fully established, memory will develop gradually. Children first remember people and objects in context though they can often be thrown by meeting someone out of context; for instance, if a child sees his grandmother in his playgroup rather than in her home it may take time to work out who she is. Later, children remember routines and incidents which had a particular impact on them.

Developing memory skills is vital not only for cognitive skills such as reading and writing but also for language skills.

ATTENTION SPAN

Children tend to have short attention spans and can be easily distracted. They flit from one activity to another as they hear interesting noises, see different toys or as people move around them. They learn over time to block out other distractions and to continue with their own activities regardless of what is going on around them. For a period they become so intent on their activities that they are difficult to distract. Later on, they develop the ability to respond to different inputs at the same time, for example they can handle verbal instructions in the middle of playing a game (Cooper, Moodley and Reynell 1978).

CONCEPT OF TIME

At first children only have a concept of 'here and now' and they want all their needs and demands met instantly. They do however develop an understanding of a sequence of actions – 'we will go to the shops and then we will go to the playground' – and of before and after. They learn the concept of present, future and past time in that order, i.e. today, then tomorrow and finally yesterday.

IMAGINATIVE PLAY

Imaginative play is when children go beyond using toys or objects for the purpose they were intended and introduce ideas into their play which come from their imagination. Although there are lots of different academic theories on the purpose of imaginative play it is clear that it has a very important place in child development. It is a useful way for children to practise their skills without fear of failure. They can try out new ideas and develop their understanding of the world, of social situations and of human relationships. By playing imaginatively, children also develop the ability to think abstractly – this box is a boat and this stick an oar – which is important for language development and for later cognitive skills. They also use it to practise talking. How often do parents hear their own words being used by children pretending to tell off a naughty teddy, or admonishing a pretend husband for being late home from work?

Children start by exploring the properties of toys. Given a toy car, a child at a very early stage of development will put it in its mouth, bang it on the floor, shake it etc. Later the child understands the function of a toy and plays with it appropriately; for example, pushing the toy car along the ground. He demonstrates imaginative play when he gets two toy cars and bashes them together saying 'crash'.

Genuine imaginative play is initiated by the child and should not be confused with play which is initiated by an adult. For instance, an adult might run the car along a track and the child might copy him or an adult might suggest that he fills the car up with some pretend petrol and he obeys. The child is not demonstrating imaginative play, just the ability to copy and understand verbal instructions.

Imaginative play

Imaginative play takes all sorts of forms. Children play using a small element of make-believe like drinking from an empty cup, or they act out roles that they have seen others perform, like a postman or a shopkeeper. Alternatively, they substitute one object for another, for example, pretending a stick is an aeroplane or a string of beads is a caterpillar or use Duplo and other building materials to create houses, cars or people.

Games and activities
General guidelines
Give your child lots of opportunities to experiment, explore and be creative with toys and objects whatever his stage of development. He will need to practise what he has learnt on as many different materials as possible and in lots of different environments so that he really understands what he is doing and why things are happening. For example, build towers with wooden bricks, beakers, barrels, soft bricks, tins of tomatoes, Tupperware boxes etc. Do it in the sitting room with bricks, in the bath with sponges and in the garden with flowerpots.

Allow your child to play with things the 'wrong' way as well as the 'right' way, because that is how he will learn. If he tries to dig sand with the wrong end of the spade let him see what happens rather than insisting that he turns the spade round. Don't over-organize him.

Chronological development

COPYING

It is impossible to make a child copy you if he does not want to or see the point. You have to start by copying him and then, as he sees the fun of it, he will start to copy you back. Copy any noises he makes like coos or raspberries. Copy any gestures he makes or any facial expressions like smiles or grimaces. If he shakes a rattle, puts bricks in a bucket or throws a toy, copy that or indeed any other spontaneous play he performs. Copy repeatedly. You will not know whether or not you are having any success until one day you find your child copying you.

Copying gestures

One Christmas when the extended family was together we all copied Charlotte lifting her arms 'up high' at meal-times. She found the sight of all these adults copying her so funny that she did it endlessly to get us to copy her. It was a major breakthrough.

There are many good rhymes to use when getting your child to copy gestures, some examples are:

If you're happy and you know it, clap your hands
If you're happy and you know it, clap your hands
If you're happy and you know it, and you really want to show it
If you're happy and you know it, clap your hands.
    Other verses:
    ... touch your nose/toes/ knees/head
    ... give a smile
    ... say 'we are'
    ... stamp your feet

Pat-a-cake, pat-a-cake, baker's man
Bake me a cake as fast as you can
Pat it and prick it and mark it with B
And bake it in the oven for baby and me.

Wind the bobbin up, wind the bobbin up
Pull pull clap clap clap
Point to the ceiling, point to the floor
Point to the window, point to the door
Clap your hands together one, two, three
Put your hands upon your knee.

The wheels on the bus go round and round, round and round, round and round
The wheels on the bus go round and round, all day long.
    Other verses:
    The bell on the bus goes ding ding ding...
    The wipers on the bus go swish swish swish...
    The horn on the bus goes beep beep beep...
    The children on the bus go up and down...
    The ladies on the bus go knit, knit, knit...

Here we go round the mulberry bush, the mulberry bush, the mulberry bush
Here we go round the mulberry bush, on a cold and frosty morning.
    Other verses:
    This is the way we brush our teeth, brush our teeth, brush our teeth...
    This is the way we comb our hair...
    This is the way we stamp our feet...
    This is the way we clap our hands...
    This is the way we wash our face...
    This is the way we wave goodbye...

I'm a little teapot, short and stout
Here's my handle, here's my spout

When you see the tea cups hear me shout
Tip me up and pour me out.

One potato, two potato, three potato, four
Five potato, six potato, seven potato, more.
(Bang one fist on the other.)

Open, shut them, open, shut them, give a little clap
Open, shut them, open, shut them, put them in your lap
Creep them, creep them, up to your little chin
Open wide your little mouth, but do not put them in.
(Use your hands in the rhyme, opening and clenching your fist.)

- Perform a simple version of Simon Says where your child copies your gestures. For example, 'Simon says put your hands on your head' or 'Simon says smile'.

- Watch nursery rhyme videos with your child and perform the actions with him.

- Children often prefer 'real activities' to mock ones so household chores are a good way of getting your child to copy you. If you are doing the dusting give him a duster, similarly give him a cloth when wiping the table. Offer him the dustpan and brush to help you sweep the floor. Get him to help empty the washing basket and load the washing machine.

- Look in a mirror, make faces and noises and see if your child will copy you.

- Try the hand-over-hand method to get your child to copy actions. Begin by guiding your child's hands to, say, pick up a brick and put it in a box. After a number of goes, as you feel him beginning to co-operate, move your hands up to his wrists. As you feel he knows what he is expected to do, move your hands up to his elbows so that you are giving less of a prompt. Eventually he may require merely a touch on the arm before being able to complete the action alone.

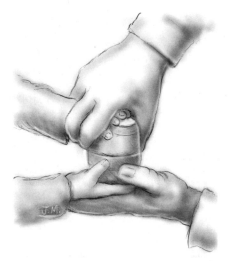

Hand-over-hand method

Other Ideas are listed in Chapter 4, p.97.

EXPLORING OBJECTS

Children need lots of opportunities to explore and experiment with as many different types of objects as they can safely use. If your child has access to a variety of things you may touch upon something which he finds particularly stimulating or interesting. You will also give him the chance to generalize his skills, make comparisons and develop his understanding.

- Do not be restricted to toys from the toy box but find objects which have different and interesting textures, shapes, colours and qualities which your child can explore and examine.

- Look around the house for everyday objects, bits of packaging, kitchen utensils, different fabrics and materials.

- Make up rattles by filling containers with rice, pasta and pulses or plastic bottles with coloured pegs, marbles, coins or water.

- Put Velcro hair rollers on a piece of felt. They make a lovely noise when pulled off.

- Let your child play with toys with different textures. You can buy some toys which incorporate different textures or make up a box or tray of objects with different qualities – sandpaper, fabrics (velvet, leather, fun fur, hessian), bubble wrap, metal, wax, wood, paper.

- Find toys with lights and sounds as they appeal to most children.

- Use toys which are easy for your child to handle initially then gradually reduce the size.

- Play with any of the objects or toys listed in Chapter 6, pp.157–159.

PICKING UP ON CUES

- Give your child as many cues as possible so that he knows what is about to happen and can therefore start to recognize a routine and make sense of the world around him.

- Warn him of what is going to happen in simple language, preferably using the same words each time.

- Use non-verbal cues; for example, place him in the bathroom so he can hear the water running for his bath; get the plastic bags out each time you go shopping or rustle cutlery noisily to signify a meal.

- You could play some music a few minutes before the end of an activity to signal that it's time to clear up.

OBJECT PERMANENCE

- Play hide and seek with a favourite toy or teddy. To begin with partially hide the toy under a cloth and ask 'Where's the teddy?' and then reveal it for your child. See if your child will find it. Once he does find it, make it harder by gradually covering more of the toy until it is totally covered.

- Hide toys under pots, beakers or containers and then reveal them or get your child to find them. Use clear pots to begin with and then coloured ones.

- When your child is in a high chair, hold a noisy toy (e.g. a rattle, bell or squeaky toy) under the tray and move it from one side to the other. Get your child to follow the noise and then pop it up every now and again to show your child. Eventually he will reach for it.

- If your child starts throwing things out of his pram or highchair, keep bringing them back to show him so that he gets the idea that they continue to exist even if he cannot see them.

- Roll marbles, cars or balls down tubes and show your child that they exist, disappear from sight and reappear at the other end.

- Play at crawling through tunnels, disappearing from sight and then reappearing.

- Play lots of peek-a-boo games with your child using a cloth or your hands to hide your face. See also Chapter 4, pp.91–2 for more ideas.

- If your child has a visual impairment, place toys slightly out of reach and get your child to search for them so that she gradually realizes that they are still there even though she cannot touch them.

EXPLORING THE ENVIRONMENT

Children need to have the opportunity to explore different and unusual environments. When children become mobile they are able to turn themselves in their cot or manoeuvre themselves into different places so that they can experience the echoes under the table and behind the sofa, feel the textures of different flooring materials, the smells in various rooms, the patterns of light and shade under a tree or a shadow passing. If your child is not mobile he may need help to experience these things.

Put your child in a variety of places, e.g. in different parts of the room – under the window, under the table, in the corner – rather than just on a rug in the middle. Vary sleeping positions and the location of the highchair at meal-times. Take him around the house with you, as you move about, to give him the opportunity to experience different rooms.

CAUSE AND EFFECT

If your child combines a lack of understanding of cause and effect with poor physical skills make sure you use toys which require a very light touch. Many commercial pop-up toys are quite stiff. Try the following ideas of toys and games which show cause and effect.

- sensory toys, for example balls that light up when bounced or squeezed, toys that vibrate or light up when a noise is made
- pop-up toys with buttons to press, slide and turn
- toys with buttons which produce lights and music
- jack-in-the-boxes
- books with buttons to press for flashing lights or noises or both
- books with flaps
- keyboards and children's tape recorders
- children's computer games
- holographic paper – put on knobs and buttons to stimulate interest in pushing and pressing
- if your child has a visual impairment, try to use toys with switches and lights.

A little bit extreme but it worked: we painted one of the memory buttons on the telephone with red nail polish and Natasha now pushes the button and phones Grandma!

RELATIONAL PLAY

Children learn how one object relates to another by having lots of opportunities to play with different things. They then learn to judge the relative size and weight of objects.

Placing one object on another

Get your child to place a smallish object on top of a large one and knock it down with a lot of noise and excitement. Then introduce all sorts of different objects so that he learns to place the object directly on top and not on the edge and to use big blocks and beakers at the bottom and smaller ones at the top.

Placing one object in another

- Use small, easily handled objects and a large shallow container like a cake tin. When the object goes in move the tin around so your child hears a nice rattling noise. Then introduce smaller containers with smaller openings. Encourage your child to move objects from one container to another.

Placing one object on another

- Use posting boxes with different shapes. If posting is difficult use tins which have soft plastic tops like marmalade, coffee or formula milk tins. Cut a hole in the top for a ping pong ball or other small object.

Rolling and sliding

Get your child to roll marbles, cars and balls down slopes, slides and tubes. Put any flat surface on an angle – a book, a tray, a piece of wood – and roll something down it. Likewise use a tube from a roll of wrapping paper or kitchen towel. Increase and decrease the angle of the slope to speed the ball up or slow it down.

Moving objects without touching them

- Line bricks up on the floor and shunt them along by pushing the last brick with another. You can use two cars to achieve the same effect.

- Encourage your child to pull cars and animals towards him by pulling on their leads rather than pulling the objects themselves. Attach a string to a favourite toy and pull it along.

- Place a drink out of reach on a piece of paper and draw the paper towards you to show your child how you can bring it within reach.

BUILDING

- Develop the ideas in 'placing one object on another' above by using more complex materials like Duplo, Stickle Bricks, blocks of different shapes – cylinders, rectangles as well as squares.
- Rather than just building towers build other shapes like walls, bridges and houses.
- Put train tracks together to make different layouts.

MATCHING, SELECTING AND NAMING

Children start matching real objects and then move on to pictures and then more abstract concepts like colour and size. It is important for children to be able to spot very tiny similarities and differences for later maths and reading skills. Think how similar an 'e' and a 'c' are.

Matching real objects

Start off with two sets of three simple everyday objects. Place one set in front of your child and then give him the other set, one by one, and get him to place each one alongside its pair. For instance, lay out an apple, spoon and brick in front of your child. As an example place the second spoon alongside the first. Then give him the apple and see if he will do the same and then finally the brick. Change the objects as he progresses.

Matching real objects

Matching pictures

In the same way, match two sets of simple pictures. Start off with a choice of three clear pictures of everyday objects and get your child to place the identical one on top. Then try more complicated pictures and more of them. Progress to very simple line drawing sketches. Use snap or lotto cards or pictures from the same book. Later you can draw your own simple sketches.

Matching shapes

Get your child to match shapes by learning to put the ball in the round hole and the cube in the square hole. Use simple posting boxes or wooden form board puzzles to match shapes like circles, squares, triangles and ovals. Initially a child will succeed by trial and error, trying each hole in turn until one goes in and will probably need a lot of help. Gradually he will learn to recognize shapes starting usually with the circle and then identifying squares, triangles and stars.

Matching symbols

Instead of matching pictures draw simple symbols on paper and get your child to match them; for example, a circle, cross and star.

Matching colours

Begin with the colours red and yellow, which are the easiest, and then move on to blue and green. Then you can introduce others.

Start by having a yellow and red bag, bucket or basket and go round the house gathering red or yellow objects and toys to put in the bags. Net bags for holding lemons and oranges are very good for this.

Try different games to get your child to match colours – build red or yellow towers, have red and yellow pieces of paper or bricks and buckets and put the relevant colours in each, match the colours in a child's tea set, thread beads of the right colour.

Matching sizes

Start with big and little and make the difference in size very obvious. Use saucepans, spoons and Tupperware containers.

Selecting and naming

Once your child is matching successfully, ask him to select the object of your choice from a group of objects. For example, have a toy car, a book and a cup in front of your child and ask him to give you the cup. Do the same with pictures, colours, shapes and sizes. Play shopping using different objects.

Finally, once your child is selecting well, ask him to name the objects, pictures, shapes etc.

SORTING AND GROUPING

Get your child to:

- Sort toys when you are tidying up so that, for example, Duplo goes in one box and books in another.

- Sort knives, forks and spoons after washing up and divide up the laundry for members of the family.

- Sort similar things to make your child look carefully, for example, buttons, beads, differently shaped shells, leaves or jigsaw puzzle pieces.

- Move on to pairing objects which go together using real objects or pictures, for example, cup and saucer, knife and fork, socks and shoes and hat and scarf.

- Group objects or pictures of objects which are used for the same purpose, for instance, sort cooking utensils from bath things or toys from clothes.

Sorting toys

PRE-NUMERACY SKILLS
Sequencing

The following games encourage children to recognize and repeat patterns as these are very important for mathematics.

Using beads or bricks, start with easy patterns using just two colours, then introduce more colours and later variations in size. Get your child to match a pattern you have made with beads, buttons or bricks using colour, size and shape. Then ask him to continue the pattern on.

One-to-one matching

Get your child to:

- Lay the table for dinner so your child places one fork with one knife or a spoon in a bowl for each person. Lay the table for a teddy bear's tea party.

One-to-one matching

- Draw a picture where your child has to connect one object with another for example a knife and fork, a dog and his lunch, animals and their young.
- Share out things like toys or food at meal-times. 'One for Robert, one for Peter...'
- Place one of four objects in each of four containers, for example, a spoon in a cup or a ball in a bowl.

Understanding the 'oneness of one'
Count things but make them tangible and physical. Handle the objects as you count them – one brick, two bricks. Start with one and two. Use things that your child can handle like bricks, balls, marbles, shoes, socks or biscuits.

When you are doing something, ask your child to give you one or two objects. For example if you are playing with Duplo ask him to give you two pieces, then one piece, then two pieces and so on.

Understanding shape and size
Play games to emphasize concepts such as large and small, long and short, light and heavy, lots and a few and full and empty. Water and sand (wet and dry) are good for many of these concepts. There are lots of books available which illustrate these concepts well.

Counting rhymes
Sing all sorts of counting rhymes to establish the sequence of numbers, for example:

> One two, buckle my shoe
> Three four, knock on my door
> Five six, pick up sticks
> Seven eight, lay them straight
> Nine ten, big fat hen.

> Five fat sausages sizzling in a pan
> One went pop and then it went bang.
> Four fat sausages...

> Five little monkeys jumping on the bed
> One fell off and bumped his head
> Mummy called the doctor and this is what he said
> 'No more monkeys jumping on the bed'.
> Four little monkeys etc.

> One two three four five
> Once I caught a fish alive
> Six seven eight nine ten
> Then I let it go again
> Why did you let it go?
> Because it bit my finger so
> Which finger did it bite?
> This little finger on the right.

Ten green bottles hanging on the wall
Ten green bottles hanging on the wall
And if one green bottle should accidentally fall
There'd be nine green bottles hanging on the wall.

One man went to mow, went to mow a meadow
One man and his dog went to mow a meadow
Two men went to mow, went...

This old man, he played one, he played nick nack on my drum
With a nick nack paddywack give the dog a bone
This old man came rolling home.
    Other verses:
    This old man he played two, he played...
    Two – shoe
    Three – tree
    Four – door
    Five – hive
    Six – on his sticks
    Seven – up in heaven
    Eight – gate
    Nine – line
    Ten – hen

One potato, two potato, three potato, four
Five potato, six potato, seven potato more.

Five currant buns in the baker's shop
Big and round, with a cherry on the top
Along came a boy with a penny one day
Bought one bun and took it right away.
Four currant buns in the baker's...

PRE-READING SKILLS

Above all, children need to develop an interest in books. Spend time together enjoying books. First of all look at bright, bold and simple picture books of familiar objects, animals and people. Children have to learn to hold them the right way round and to 'read' them from left to right.

Developing an enjoyment of books

Then move on to very simple story books where people are performing actions – for example, a day's routine or a shopping trip – so that he gets the idea of a sequence of events.

- Get your child to find a particular picture in a book or a specific book.

- Encourage your child to interact with the book, for example by pretending to eat the food in the picture, kiss the doll, cut the cake with a knife or pat the dog.

- Children need to learn that writing means something. Try to show that you can read the words in books, in cards, on signs and on shopping lists.

- Rhymes and rhythms all help children's language and reading skills so sing and say lots of nursery rhymes and songs. Get your child to fill in words or to predict what is going to happen next.

- Find 'spot the difference' puzzles where your child has to point out the differences between a set of two pictures.

All the matching skills mentioned above on pp.70–71 are vital. Children need to have quite detailed visual discrimination to differentiate between letters. Once children can match symbols you can start getting them to match letters, numbers and words.

- Write out two words like 'car' and 'television' on cards and get your child to match another card saying 'television'.

- Put names on bedroom doors, by place mats and on pegs so that your child sees them around the house. His own name and those of his family will probably be the first words he recognizes.

- Create a photograph album with pictures of family members and write their names next to them. Play matching games. Write out the names on individual cards. First get your child to match the word to the word and picture. Then cover up the picture and match it just to the word. Finally get your child to match the word to the picture only.

- Stick the names of objects on the objects themselves and play a matching or fetching game. For example, stick the words 'door', 'television', 'chair' and 'teddy' on the relevant object and give your child a second sticker which he has to place with the first sticker. Alternatively get him to bring you the matching sticker. 'Post-it' notes are good for this.

Because developing memory is also vital for pre-reading skills, play the games given below in the section on Memory p.79.

PRE-WRITING SKILLS

Once your child is making marks on paper, play games which encourage greater accuracy and the idea of tracing figures on paper.

- Play with road map floor-mats and encourage your child to trace the journey of the car or with train sets where children push the train along the track.

- Get your child to play with a bead and wire maze where he moves the beads along the wires to get them to the other end.

- Make patterns in sand and encourage your child to copy you.

- Draw two points on a piece of paper – for example, two shoes, a dog and his dinner, or patches of colour, letters or numbers. Get your child to join them with a line.

- Encourage your child to draw lines going up and down or across the page.

- Draw two parallel lines across the page about an inch or two apart and see if your child will draw lines from left to right within the lines.

- Draw wide lines in a fluorescent pen and get your child to trace the lines with his pencil. Make the lines wide and straight initially then narrower, with curves, zigzags and ultimately quite complex.

- Draw two cars and a wide road linking them. Get your child to draw the journey following the road. At first make the road straight then with angular bends, and finally curvy.

- Get your child to copy simple figures like a circle, cross and T or to trace over them.

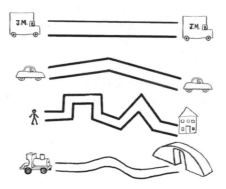

Draw the journey

Colouring

Initially, children colour the whole piece of paper, but you gradually want them to gain the control to colour smaller and more specific sections.

Start by getting your child to colour in a large piece of paper and then give him a smaller piece. Try placing the paper on a piece of black card so that he keeps the marks to the paper. Then introduce easy pictures for him to colour in, for instance an outline of a circle, car, train or person. Make the edge very thick and the picture a reasonable size but not fiddly so your child does not get bored too quickly. Then reduce the size of the picture and get your child to colour within its boundaries.

You could try raising the edge of the picture so that he cannot go over the edge of it (this is particularly useful if your child is visually impaired). Glue some string around the edge of the picture or use glue that dries in a solid raised line.

Look at Chapter 5, pp.146–147 for further ideas for games.

Parallel development

MEMORY

- Read a very simple story to your child a few times and ask him to tell you what happens next.

- Singing nursery rhymes and action songs is a good way of improving memory as children will fill in the last word or remember some of the key words. If they are not talking they may be able to show that they remember what happens by using the action or sign.

- Ask your child to tell you what has happened during the day or talk to him about what has happened.

- Ask your child to get things out or to put things away in the correct place.

- Play pairs with cards. Place pairs of cards face down and get each player to turn over two cards. If they are a pair, the player can remove them, if not they are replaced.

- Play a version of lotto, by placing the cards face down in front of you and turning a card over in turn. If you turn one over which fits on your board you can pick it up and the first person to complete his board wins.

- Try a very simple version of the traditional party game where you place two or three objects on a tray, handle them and name them. Then cover them up and ask your child to name them or, alternatively, take something away and ask your child what is missing.

EXTENDING ATTENTION SPANS

- Don't be unrealistic in your expectations. All small children have a short attention span which develops over time.

- Finish all activities, even if it means you complete a game very quickly, to give the idea that your child should work through his activities to the end.

- Remove distractions as far as possible (see Chapter 2, pp.36–37).

- Don't make activities too difficult but do make them fun so that your child will want to do them and will not be frustrated by his lack of ability.

- Establish appropriate places for doing things – eating at the table, sitting down to paint etc.

- Play with cause and effect games, see pp.67–68 to encourage your child to spend time exploring toys to see what happens.

- Play games where your child has to wait for a moment, rather than get immediate satisfaction. For example, say 'ready, steady, go' or 'one, two, three' and then roll a ball or push a car or knock something down.

- Blow bubbles and make your child wait for a moment before blowing more.

- Find an activity your child enjoys and seek to extend it very gradually, either by continuing the play or by introducing one new element to keep the idea going until just before your child gets bored. For example, if he has a train set start by laying out the track, put the train on, then add a driver, carriages, put things in the carriages, make a bridge, make a station, get the train to stop and change passengers.

- Alternatively try lots of short activities in quick succession but maintaining concentration.

- Use a book like 'Ketchup on Your Cornflakes?' by Nick Sharratt (published by Picture Hippos) where you ask lots of questions like 'Do you like ketchup on your toothbrush?', 'Do you like ketchup on your toes?' and 'Do you like ketchup in your bath?' requiring a 'No' before you reach 'Do you like ketchup on your chips?' 'Yes'.

Listening skills are also closely associated with attention span, as children later need to be able to concentrate on a task and listen to others at the same time. You could try some of the listening games listed in Chapter 6, pp.159–162.

CONCEPT OF TIME

Children only gradually gain an understanding of the passing of time. However, it is worth trying to help them to understand if only because it can be a source of great frustration and unhappiness when children want to do something 'now' and cannot.

- An understanding of a sequence of events must come first. So in daily life explain the sequence of events. For example, first you are going to tidy up and then you will have lunch. Keep it simple and repeat it frequently.

- Show sequences of actions when reading a book or when playing with dolls and teddies.

- Give a timetable verbally each day maybe for half a day at a time. 'We are going to have breakfast, then we are going to go and see George and Martha.'

- Point out clocks in books and around the house and talk about it being 'time for drinks', 'time for school'.

- Use a visual timetable to show sequences and give your child an understanding of his day. See Chapter 2, pp.49–51 for details.

IMAGINATIVE PLAY

Once your child is copying actions and activities, try to extend his play so that he introduces some pretend elements. For example, get him to drink using an empty cup or comb his hair using a toy comb. Children start to play imaginatively either by pretending that their dolls are doing familiar activities with real objects (like sitting on the toilet) or by performing real actions but using obvious toys (making a cup of tea with a toy tea set).

Start with the simplest level of pretend play and extend it gradually by one element at a time so that you are getting a variety of actions and sequences of actions.

Gather a few toys together so you can 'pretend play' everyday activities on a doll or teddy. For instance have a teddy and real examples of a cup, spoon, bowl, comb, blanket, rattle. Play appropriately with the articles and get your child to do the same. Move on to using toy articles instead of real ones.

Later on use other toys which reflect your child's interests, for example:

- cooking – with real or toy implements
- eating/feeding – himself or toys
- cars – with a toy car going shopping, to the petrol station, for a drive
- houses – using a very large box or a sheet draped over a clothes horse or chairs
- shops – with a basket or bag and tins or packets of food, vegetables and fruit plus a till with money
- dressing-up box with your old clothes, shoes, hats and accessories
- baby – with a doll and cot, nappies etc.
- postman delivering letters on foot or in a car.

As you play sometimes pretend that one object is in fact another. You could pick up a stick and pretend it is a dog or use a box as a car.

CHAPTER 4

Language Development

The theory
What is language development?

Children learn to hear and understand what is being said to them, to copy the sounds back and then to use the words in different formations as speech. However, language is much more than speech alone. We all learn to understand body language and gesture and to pick up on the nuances of eye contact in order to communicate more effectively (Wells 1985; Law 1994).

Chronological development

THE NEWBORN BABY

A newborn baby is unable to survive on her own so she has to communicate in some way to make sure her needs are met. A baby cries to communicate that she needs a feed, is uncomfortable or wants some companionship. Although a newborn baby does not seek eye contact, she does not avoid it. In fact, she is more interested in faces than anything else. Sometimes a baby can show that she can copy adult gestures very early, for example copying an adult by sticking out her tongue.

EYE CONTACT

Babies soon learn to make eye contact because it is through communicating with people that they will be cared for and learn about themselves and the world about them. Making eye contact is fundamental to language development. Children have to look at people's faces to understand about communication, to pick up on the idea of taking turns to talk and to detect the emotion which people show in their eyes and facial expressions.

Eye contact

SMILING AND VOCALIZING

Babies learn to smile. It is their first way of communicating apart from crying and they soon discover that it gets a good response from adults around them.

Children learn to make a greater range of sounds than just crying as they develop control over the muscles of the lips, tongue and larynx. They laugh, chuckle and squeal. They coo, blow bubbles, gurgle and trill. These noises are precursors to speech.

TURN-TAKING

As a child starts to vocalize, she also starts to take turns with an adult. It usually starts off being barely perceptible. When holding or feeding a baby a mother will intuitively have a conversation. The baby makes a noise and the mother will copy her making a noise or silly face back, the baby then responds with gurgles, coos and attempts at copying. The child learns to 'say something', wait for a reply, then to 'say something' further and again wait for a response. This is the basis for conversations – the idea of taking turns and of picking up on body language and facial expression to know when to talk and when to be quiet. It is a vital skill but not an obvious one that parents usually notice.

BABBLING

Children continue to learn to make further sounds as they practise more with their throat and mouth, and later as they start to eat solid food and chew.

The noises children make will partly depend on the position they are placed in. A child who is lying on her back will only be able to make vowel sounds in the back of her throat (aagh) whereas a child who is sitting upright will be able to make consonant sounds at the front of her mouth (baba, dada, mama) called babbling. Babbling is the range of sounds involving consonants and vowels. Children go on to use them in long strings – for example dadadada.

COPYING

Copying is fundamental to all learning and is particularly important in the development of language skills. This is because it is by copying the sounds they hear that children learn to make single words, and later to learn phrases and put together more complex sentences. Children learn to copy gestures and sounds at about the same time. They start to wave and clap in imitation of others and to copy noises if not words, especially animal noises such as moo and baa.

UNDERSTANDING

Children learn to understand that a picture of a car represents a real car. When they see a picture of a car they realize it is actually a representation of the four-wheeled beast in the driveway and is not just a squiggle on a piece of paper. They then go on to understand that 'sounds', i.e. words, can symbolize or represent an actual object. When we hear the sound 'dog', it is not just a noise: we visualize a furry animal with four legs and waggy tail.

Children pick up on the fact that sounds are words and have meanings from hearing the same words repeated again and again so that eventually they make the association. Whenever the dog appears Daddy says 'dog' and so the child associates the word with the animal. Children therefore first understand words for familiar objects and people which they hear repeatedly and which are concrete and not abstract. Children will recognize their own names and also the words they hear most often like bye bye, no, mummy, daddy, siblings' names etc. There is a remarkable consistency in the first words understood and said by children across families, races and cultures.

Children show they understand what is being said by responding to simple questions like 'Where's the cat?' by eye pointing, gesturing or pointing with their finger. They will also start to obey simple instructions like 'Give me the drink' or 'Come here'.

Children understand quite a wide range of words before they are able to 'say' anything.

JARGON

Children start to talk to themselves in a sing-songy way called jargon. They copy the intonation patterns of a conversation with word-like combinations and a range of sounds but it is not recognizable and has no meaning.

PRE-VERBAL COMMUNICATION

Before they learn to speak children learn to communicate by other means. They eye point by looking in the direction of something they want, such as an apple, a drink or a particular toy. They then gesture with their whole hand and later point with their index finger towards what they want.

Children learn to use natural gestures to communicate, for instance a child will wave bye bye before she learns to say it and she will learn to raise her arms up high if she wants to be lifted up or out of her cot before she can say 'up'.

FIRST WORDS

Often a child's first word will be a 'symbolic' noise, for example, brmm brmm, moo, woof, choo choo.

First words are quite often incomprehensible to anyone but the child's own parents who will have picked up from the context that 'bibi' is used consistently to mean 'biscuit' and 'bu' means 'bus' (starting a word but not finishing it is a common feature at this stage).

First words are usually labels for people, particularly family members, animals and objects. Children then learn words for food and clothing. Often the first family name used will be that of the second carer rather than the first, since he or she is probably mentioned by name more often. If the mother is the primary carer, rather than talk about herself she will probably talk about 'Daddy' as in 'Daddy's gone to work' or 'Daddy's home'.

A child may use a single 'word' to mean a whole phrase, for example 'Daddy' could mean 'Daddy's gone', 'here's Daddy' or 'I want

Daddy' and the meaning will be impossible to comprehend without the context.

First words can often be used very loosely so that all men are called 'Daddy', all vehicles 'car' and all animals 'cats'.

TWO WORDS

Children not only expand their vocabulary so that they know more words but they also start to use them in combination with others so that they can express more complex statements. 'More juice', 'Daddy gone' are common starting points. Again the exact meaning may often only be clear from the context.

Children are interested in the present (they do not develop an understanding of the past and future until later), in objects, in people – especially those close to them – in their routines, food, clothes, animals and transport. These topics will therefore be the subjects of most conversations.

Combining a noun and verb is the classic two-word combination which is the basis for further language development – man walking, dog eating, boy running. Children also combine an adjective and noun – big car, red bus.

THREE WORDS

From a two-word combination involving a noun and verb children add a further noun so they will start saying 'girl drinks milk', 'farmer drives tractor'.

BEYOND THREE WORDS

After children have developed the ability to use three words in combination they start developing a more grammatical structure to their language in the following way:

- They ask what and who questions and use pronouns such as I, me and you.
- They start using more pronouns (e.g. him and her), plurals (horses, glasses) and prepositions (in, on, under). They carry out simple conversations and can talk about the past and present. They start asking where questions.
- They ask why, when and how questions.

By the time they start school children's speech is usually grammatically and phonetically correct.

LANGUAGE DELAY OR LANGUAGE DISORDER
Some children with special needs follow the usual development pattern but at a slower pace and this is called a language delay. Other children, however, often with an autism diagnosis, do not follow the usual pattern. They may skip earlier elements such as eye contact and turn-taking but be quick to develop spoken language. This is called a language disorder. If your child has a language disorder it is still very important to concentrate on the early skills such as eye contact and understanding one word because these are still vital to the development of functional language skills.

Parallel development

USES OF LANGUAGE
Children initially use language to make comments on what they can see: 'Look car' and to ask for things they need and want: 'Biscuit'. Gradually they use language not only in longer forms (more words) but with more complexity and flexibility to ask questions – 'Where's Daddy?'; to request information – 'Why is it raining?'; to request attention – 'How do you do this?' and to negotiate with others – 'You pull this string and I'll pull that one'.

PRONUNCIATION
Children develop the ability over time to make different sounds, to distinguish between all the different sounds they hear and to be able to pronounce all consonants correctly. At school age children may still be confusing some sounds such as s, f, and th.

ATTENTION SPANS
In parallel with the development of language, children learn to extend their attention spans. When they are very young, children are initially very easily distracted from what they are doing. If they are playing with a game but see an interesting doll they will immediately transfer their attention.

They later become fixated on one activity, learn to cut out all distractions and will not tolerate any intervention because they cannot cope with doing two things at once.

Gradually they become able to cope with doing an activity and having someone give information and advice at the same time. They are able to do their task and at the same time listen to simple and relevant instructions. Later they can switch their attention between their activity and more complex instructions (see Chapter 3, pp.59–60).

Games and activities
General guidelines
Below are some pointers for ways to make it easier for your child to understand you.

- Speak simply and clearly. Don't wrap up important words in lots of flowery language but use the important words on their own. Make it easy for your child to get the message. Don't say 'I would rather you didn't bang that knife on the table', say 'No banging'. Don't say 'Why don't you put the brick in the bucket?', say 'Brick in'.

- Make your language fit your child's level of understanding and just be one step beyond. So if she uses one word, use two and encourage her to use two back. Adapt your language as your child progresses.

- Repeat simple phrases and words over and over again at every opportunity.

- Babies and children respond to a high-pitched voice which is why adults use it naturally. Don't stop using this voice even though your child is no longer a small baby.

- Talk to your child with an interesting, sing-songy voice. Vary your tone to maintain your child's attention. A flat, monotonous tone is very dull.

- Make sure your facial expressions and tone of voice give the same message as your language. Communication is more complex than just understanding the spoken word. We all listen to tone and interpret body language as well as the words themselves in order to understand the full message we are being given. Children are no different and if they are finding communication a problem it does not help them if you are saying 'no' very forcefully with a big grin on your face. (Later children will learn to deal with mixed messages.)

- Use natural gesture when you speak as it will aid understanding.

- Respond immediately to any communication your child makes with you whether it be a smile, a gesture or a word. Make her understand that communication works.

- Don't overcorrect your child because it will tend to make her shy of attempting new words and language. Just say 'yes' and repeat back what your child was trying to say. For example if your child says 'bibi' for biscuit say 'Yes, biscuit'.

- Sing to your child. Children and adults have an innate musicality and it is worth taking advantage of it. Some children who do not respond to the spoken word will respond much better when they have instructions or information sung to them.

- Speech therapists say that 'please' and 'thank you' are not useful words in terms of communication and should only be introduced once a child has a fairly extensive vocabulary. There is nothing more unhelpful than a situation where a child is asked what she wants and she just says 'please'. She should first be taught drink, toilet, food, biscuit, and so on.

- Current lifestyles of car seats, outward facing pushchairs, wall-to-wall children's TV and computers mean that children spend far less time looking at their parents from a pram as they walk to the shops or following them around the house with a duster. Nothing can replace person–person stimulation for learning language and social skills. Make sure you still spend lots of time talking to your child, playing with her and involving her in household and day to day activities like shopping, cleaning, sorting the laundry and cooking. You may not find it exciting but it is how she will learn to interact and communicate.

- If your child has a hearing impairment but no other delay, consult a speech therapist or adviser for the hearing impaired for the best approach to communication development.

Chronological development

EYE CONTACT

If your child does not make eye contact readily then work on it. Even if she already has more advanced skills, it is important that she makes good eye contact in order to learn language.

You must always try to be directly in front of and close to your child so that she cannot avoid your gaze. If necessary get down to her level. Remember you are much bigger than her. Crouch down or lie down on the floor. Move yourself, not your child. Never physically force her to look at you even though you may have to work very hard for her attention.

Always aim to get eye contact before starting any new game or activity. Once you have got eye contact, reward it immediately with the new toy or game.

Make your face 'interesting' for your child so that she wants to look at you. If she just sees a blank and bored expression she won't be tempted, but she might be if you make an over the top effort. You could:

- give lots of big smiles
- make silly faces – waggle your eyebrows, screw up your face
- make silly noises
- wear unusual hats, glasses (large, colourful or silly), sunglasses, dangly earrings or a red nose
- wear masks
- use face paints.

Sometimes you can attract a child's attention by blowing softly on her cheek or by being very still and silent. A change may gain more attention than lots of frenetic activity.

Take an object that has caught your child's attention and bring it to your face. Her eyes will usually follow it. Reward the eye contact by playing with the toy and then build on your success by doing it again with the same or a different toy.

Alternatively, you can hide a toy behind your head, wait for eye contact and then show the toy. Use a favourite toy, the spoon at meal-times or a squeaky toy where you have the added interest of a noise.

Play peek-a-boo games using:

- scarves (ordinary or chiffon/semi-transparent)
- teatowels in the kitchen
- towels in the bathroom
- sheets when changing bedlinen
- washing on the line

- curtains
- furniture and doors
- clothes when getting dressed and undressed
- bibs when pulling them on and off
- your hands on your child's face and on your own
- your child's hands on her face and your own.

When playing peek-a-boo sing the following using a scarf to hide your child:

> I can play peek-a-boo
> Are you there? Yes I am
> Are you there? Yes I am
> Peek-a peek-a peek-a peek-a booooo.

Sing songs with your child sitting on your knee and looking directly at you. For instance:

> Row, row, row your boat gently down the stream
> Merrily, merrily, merrily, merrily life is but a dream.

> See-saw Margery Daw
> Johnny shall have a new master
> He shall have but a penny a day
> Because he can't work any faster.

> Horsey, horsey don't you stop
> Just let your feet go clippety clop
> Your tail goes swish and your wheels go round
> Giddy up we're homeward bound.

> This is the way the ladies ride
> Trot trot trot
> This is the way the farmer rides
> Hobble dee hoy, Hobble dee hoy
> This is the way the plough boys ride
> A-gallop a-gallop and into the ditch.
> (Or one of the hundreds of different versions.)
> (Bounce your child up and down and 'drop' her when you go 'into the ditch'.)

> Bumpty bumpty bumpty bump
> As if I was riding my charger
> Bumpty bumpty bumpty bump
> As proud as an Indian Rajah
> All the girls declare

That I'm a gay old stager
Hey, hey clear the way
Here comes the galloping major.

Have you ever ever ever in your long legged life
Seen a long legged sailor with a long legged wife
No I've never never never in my long legged life
Seen a long legged sailor with a long legged wife.
(Lay your child flat on her back and hold her legs by the ankles moving
them backwards and forwards, with knees bent, rather like a cycling
motion.)

Join a child who is engaging in solitary play by mirroring her actions with
the same or similar toys. Use some language but do not be afraid of
silence.

WAITING

As a forerunner to turn-taking games try to extend your child's concentration so she is made to wait, even if it is for seconds, rather than have
an instant response. For example:

- Play games where a ball or car goes down a tube and
  reappears a few moments later.

- Blow bubbles so that your child has to wait a few moments for
  the next one to appear.

CAUSE AND EFFECT IN COMMUNICATION

It is important to engage your child in early interactions so that she
realizes that she can have an effect on other people. If she makes a
face, her parent will make a face back. She will become aware then
that communication is a two-way process. Usually parents instinctively
and unconsciously copy any little facial movements their baby makes
and the baby quickly learns to copy them back or initiate games
because she likes the response and the reward of the attention.
However, because children with special needs can be slow to pick this
up, parents can feel they are wasting their time and give up because of
the lack of response. Look out for any mouth movements or faces that
your child makes (such as opening and closing her mouth or sticking out
her tongue) and respond promptly by copying her so that she sees the
effect she has. Even though you may not get a response immediately, it
is important to keep persevering as it is a vital skill underpinning subse-
quent development.

- Sit your child on your knee or opposite you and watch for any faces your child makes and then respond similarly. Give an exaggerated response and then wait for her again. Meal-times or quiet times are also good for picking up on any communication attempts your child might make.

- Use the ideas in Promoting early interactive conversations on pp.109–11 below as they are addressing the same issue.

TURN-TAKING

Remember that children with special needs can take a long time to respond so always give your child longer to reply than you feel is natural. When you think she is not going to take her turn remember to count to ten again to give her extra time.

- Build on the ideas in cause and effect above. Sit opposite your child and copy any facial expressions or sounds your child makes, see if she copies any of your facial movements. Try to extend any 'conversation' into a turn-taking game of watching, waiting and then copying.

- Roll a ball or push a car to your child and get her to return it to you. If you do it sitting opposite each other at a table, it is good for eye contact too.

- You can turn many games into turn-taking games, for example putting things into a container, posting shapes, drawing or completing a puzzle. Choose something that your child enjoys.

Taking turns to put oranges in a bowl

- Take turns when feeding animals, either a pet or on a children's farm.

UNDERSTANDING THAT LANGUAGE MEANS SOMETHING

Children have to learn that the sounds they hear have meaning. The following games help a child to learn that words indicate that something interesting is going to happen!

Anticipation rhymes and songs

Use the appropriate actions to go with the following rhymes and songs.

Tickling games

> Round and round the garden like a teddy bear
> One step, two steps and tickle you under there.
>
> This little piggy went to market, this little piggy stayed at home
> This little piggy had roast beef and this little piggy had none
> And this little piggy cried wee wee wee all the way home.

Knee rides

> Humpty Dumpty sat on the wall, Humpty Dumpty had a great fall
> All the king's horses and all the king's men couldn't put Humpty together again.
>
> Walk walk walk trot trot trot canter canter canter and over the fence.
> (Bounce your child up high when you go 'over the fence'.)
>
> This is the way the ladies ride...
> (For the words see p.92)
>
> Ring a ring o' roses
> A pocketful of posies
> A tishoo, a tishoo
> We all fall down.
> Fishes in the water
> Fishes in the sea
> We all jump up
> With a one two three.
>
> The grand old duke of York, he had ten thousand men
> He marched them up to the top of the hill and he marched them down again
> And when they were up they were up
> And when they were down they were down
> And when they were only half way up they were neither up nor down.

In the swimming pool

The swimming pool is a good place for doing rhymes like:

- 'Humpty Dumpty' (sit your child on the side of the swimming pool and get her to jump in at the right moment)
- 'Ring a ring o' roses' (hold your child in your arms and fall down then jump up)
- 'The wheels on the bus' (making movements in the water, blowing bubbles for the bell, bounce your child up and down etc.)
- 'Down in the water, down in the sea, playing with the fishes, one two three'.

You can also do lots of jumping 'in', getting 'out', jumping 'up' and 'down'.

Ready, steady, go

Play 'Ready, steady, go' games because they will teach your child that 'go' means something is going to happen. For example, say 'Ready, steady, go' and then roll a ball, push a car, push your child fast in her pushchair or knock a brick tower down. Just make something exciting happen. Increase the pause between 'steady' and 'go' to maximize anticipation and increase concentration. Then you can encourage your child to perform the action instead of you, so you say 'ready, steady, go' and she knocks down the bricks or throws the ball.

Sing to your child

Find a tune that you like, for example 'Here we go round the mulberry bush' or 'The farmer's in his den' and make up your own words to suit the occasion. 'This is the way we do the puzzle', 'This is the way we eat our yoghurt', 'Nick is on the bed', 'Christopher's doing a poo'. It becomes very easy and it is also a good way of easing tension. Children love 'live music' and cannot distinguish between you and Pavarotti. So sing as badly as you like and do not feel embarrassed.

> If Ruby wants more of something and cannot have it, she gets very upset but singing 'no more' instead of saying it calms her and me down and usually makes us all smile.

Use exaggerated language like 'Noooooo' instead of 'No' to make language more interesting and more understandable.

COPYING

Children learn to copy you by first seeing you copy them.

To encourage your child to copy sounds you make you first have to copy the sounds she makes. She will then learn to copy you back. When your child makes noises such as coos or gurgles or makes faces, copy them back to her.

At other times make the sounds you have heard your child making, whatever they are, and see if she will copy you back. Pushchair walks, car journeys and bath-times are good times because children are more able to concentrate and less likely to be distracted.

Use natural gestures frequently and see if your child will copy them. For example wave goodbye, say 'shhh' with your finger to your lips, put a hand up to your ear for 'listen', put your fingers to your nose for 'pooey nappy'.

Also see Chapter 3, pp.62–64 for other games to encourage copying skills.

ENCOURAGING SOUNDS

Children vary as to when they are most vocal. Some children are most vocal during or after a meal when muscles have been exercised, some like the bath where noises are exaggerated, and others are most vocal in the car or pushchair when they are not distracted by other things. Follow their lead. Children need to develop the muscles of the mouth and throat to make a full range of sounds. So, although some of these ideas may not appear to be related to making sounds, they are nevertheless important for strengthening different muscles.

- Tickling and laughing games – a chuckle and laugh are a baby's next way of communicating after crying and smiling.

- Make funny noises and faces to your child and encourage her to copy. If she responds reward her exaggeratedly.

- While both of you are looking at yourselves in a mirror, try to get your child to copy your facial expressions and noises.

- Play games involving blowing. Blow through straws into water, play blow football or move pieces of tissue paper by blowing through a straw. Blow musical instruments like mouth organs, whistles, party whistles, kazoos, pipes, recorders and trumpets. See what happens if you blow flimsy scarves, feathers, bubbles, light mobiles, pieces of ripped up paper and tissues. Blow out birthday cake candles. Blow bubbles under the water in the bath or swimming pool. Blow dandelion clocks in the summer.

Blowing bubbles

- Get your child to suck on straws for drinking or use straws to pick up paper fish, Smarties, peas etc.
- Get your child to lick things like stickers, stamps and envelopes. Encourage her to lick food from around her mouth. Get her to lick ice-creams and lollies.
- Eating chewy and lumpy food gets all the jaw muscles working and increases the range of sounds a child can make so you should encourage your child to move from puréed food to lumpy food. If your child has a problem eating lumpy or chewy food then you should consult your speech therapist.
- As you play and read books make lots of symbolic sounds – brmm brmm, moo, woof, miaow, baa, tick tock, clip clop etc. – because these are often the first meaningful sounds a child will make.
- Play games your child enjoys, then stop and wait for her to show that she wants more by vocalizing. Say 'more' or 'again' and repeat the game. Find a game that is really motivating for your child. It might be tickling, singing or rough and tumble games.
- Sing rhymes such as the following:

Row row row your boat gently down the stream
If you see a crocodile don't forget to scream. Aaaaaagh! (get your
child to say Aaaagh)

Hey diddle diddle, the cat and the fiddle
The cow jumped over the moon
The little dog laughed
HA! (get child to laugh before continuing)
To see such fun
And the dish ran away with the spoon.

- Try humming songs like lullabies.

Natasha had a protruding tongue from birth and for three years
only vocalized 'ee' with her mouth wide open and tongue sticking
out. We tried everything to bring her lips together such as massag-
ing her mouth, putting a finger under her chin to encourage the
swallowing reflex, telling her to close her mouth and experimenting
with all sorts of food on her lips. One day I lay on a bean bag and
put Natasha on my tummy. There was some gentle piped music on
the cassette in the background. I started to hum and all of a sudden
Natasha started humming too. Six months later she can say baa
baa and mama.

- You can buy or borrow mobiles which move or toys which
  vibrate when a sound is made. They give children a wonderful
  incentive to make sounds.

EARLY COMMUNICATION SKILLS
Try to think of language as communication rather than just speaking.
Everyone hopes speech will come but it may take time so you and your
child need to find other ways to communicate. This will enable your child
to develop all her skills and relieve some of the frustration you will both
feel if your child cannot express her needs and desires. In addition,
improving pre-language skills will increase the chances that language
will develop. If her speech is delayed, be sensitive to the other ways in
which she is actually communicating and encourage her. If she sees the
advantages of communicating she is much more likely to want to learn
to speak.

- All attempts and efforts to communicate should be rewarded
  with lots of praise and encouragement to begin with. If you
  think your child might be trying to communicate by some

means, perhaps eye pointing (i.e. looks specifically at something, see pp.85–86) or vocalizing, give her the benefit of the doubt.

- Respond immediately to what your child is communicating to show that you are interested and understand her. If she eye points at a book offer her the book. If she vocalizes at the sight of the cat say 'Yes, it's the cat'. If she is asking for something, you don't have to say 'yes' all the time but you should acknowledge that she is trying to communicate and not ignore her, otherwise she might not be so keen to 'talk'.

Emma's third sign was biscuit and we were delighted. Obviously we rewarded her with a biscuit each time so that she saw the benefits of communicating. However, after five biscuits (even broken into hundreds of fragments) we did have to start saying 'no'!

- Always reinforce what your child is trying to tell you by saying it back. For example if your child eye points at a drink or brings a cup to you respond by saying 'Mia wants a drink? Here's the drink'.
- Don't anticipate your child's every need. Give her the opportunity to make a request, point to a toy on a high shelf, show she is hungry or demand a change. If you anticipate her all the time there will be no need for communication.

The following are ways in which children communicate before they have speech.

Crying
A baby expresses her unhappiness by crying and parents learn to understand what their child's needs are by the nature of her cry. It might be food, a nappy change, wind, sleep or cuddles. Children with a communication problem may use this method for some time, as it is effective.

Early communication skills

Laughing

By laughing children are also communicating that they are having fun and enjoying themselves. Parents naturally want to repeat actions which get a good response from their child.

Signs of anticipation

An early form of communication is showing signs of anticipation. For example, children start wriggling when they hear the first words of tickling songs and knee rides because they know something fun is going to happen.

Eye pointing

Children use eye pointing to express their needs or respond to questions but parents have to be quite sensitive to pick it up. If you ask your child to show you the picture of the dog, she may not point with her finger but may look at the dog instead. This shows that she understands you and is responding to you. Similarly, your child may eye point to things around the house that she wants. If your child is sitting on your knee looking at a book, it is difficult to pick up on eye pointing, so it may be worth sitting opposite her.

Pointing

Children point with their finger or gesture with their whole hand to indicate their needs or respond to a request. They also point generally as a way of getting you to tell them about the world and interact with them. To encourage pointing as a way of communicating try the following:

- Hold a toy or food slightly out of reach and encourage your child to reach for it or point to it to show she wants it.
- Sing 'Wind the bobbin up' with appropriate gestures (see Chapter 3, p.63 for the words).
- Play teasing games where you offer your child a toy and then pull it away as she reaches for it.
- Try holding your child's hand in yours and pointing at pictures in books.
- Have pictures of things your child likes, for example, food at meal-times or toys when you are playing, and ask her to point to what she wants.

Liam's main difficulty has been the acquisition and use of language, but we have found that he can ask for what he wants using pictures. I photographed a great number of familiar household objects, toys and things he particularly liked, had them laminated and Velcroed them to a board which we hang on the kitchen door. Now he can bring the picture as his way of asking for something. The only problem we had with this was that for a while every time he walked past the board he would select the biscuit picture! We now leave that one off the board if he asks too much. This has been a big help to Liam and us.

For other ideas see Chapter 5, pp.141–142.

The direct approach
If children cannot communicate verbally they often bring you the actual object to tell you what they want. If your child brings a book it probably means 'read to me', an empty cup means 'I'm thirsty'.

Children take adults by the hand and lead them to what they want. Sometimes they may take your hand and place it on the relevant object. It is a very effective way of communicating if your child has not got the language to say 'Please could you get the puzzle out of the cupboard for me?'

Gestures
Children use natural gesture to communicate. For example, they might show that they want to be lifted up by raising their hands. Use natural gesture to accompany your normal speech.

SIGNING SYSTEMS

A natural extension of gesture is to introduce signs. Young children with communication problems are often introduced to Makaton or Signalong which are signing systems in which the spoken word is accompanied by a sign. The signs are derived from British Sign Language and some have been modified to be expressive and clear with large arm movements rather than small fiddly ones. Children therefore learn language in a multi-sensory way. They hear the word spoken and they see a sign which provides a visual reinforcement. They can communicate back either with the word if they can say it, or with the sign, or both.

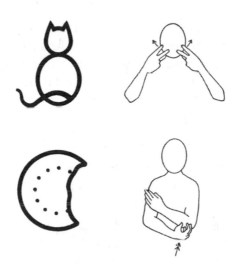

Makaton symbol and sign for cat and biscuit

Many parents fear that if their child learns to sign she will never speak but this is certainly not the case. All the evidence suggests that signs aid speech. Although it is impossible to prove the success or otherwise of such systems, research has shown that children use the signs while they need to and when they can say the words they automatically drop the signs. Some children use Makaton or Signalong for a very short period and then start speaking; some use it for a long time and find it really helpful; while for others it does not seem to make a difference.

Both Makaton and Signalong only sign the most important words in a sentence, not each and every word. For example if you asked 'Do you want a drink?' you could just sign 'drink'.

We found Makaton to be a life-saver. Christopher first learnt to sign 'drink' and 'bird' at about two years old. He learnt 'biscuit' and 'more' at about two and a half and from about three his vocabulary exploded. He doesn't need Makaton so much to understand what people are saying but it is his only way to express himself. At four however he has just begun to vocalize. Before he could sign he showed considerable frustration, anger and unhappiness but they have been relieved to an extent by signing. His younger brother Nicholas started signing when he was one and I must admit I panicked momentarily but as he learns to say the words he drops the signs and his combination of words and signs make him extremely communicative.

Makaton and Signalong have a somewhat different approach to each other but they share the same basic idea. Makaton is more widely used but it tends to depend on where you live and it is worth finding out which system is used in your area so that you work in harmony with your child's speech therapist and school. See Chapter 11, pp.256 and 262 for more details of both organizations.

How to use signs with your child

Makaton and Signalong run courses on their signing systems which are vital if you plan to use signs but if you want to start straightaway, ask someone to show you some signs.

- Select three or four words which are most relevant to your child. Choose words which your child will be motivated to understand and use back, for example: drink, biscuit, more and dog. There is not much point teaching her cigarette, boss or work. Learn the signs and don't feel self-conscious about using them everywhere and anywhere.

- Whenever you use the chosen words in your conversation give the sign too. Get everyone who cares for your child to do the same – friends, grandparents, playgroups.

- Always say the words when you use the signs, they are not a replacement for speech.

- Make sure your child is looking at you when you sign otherwise you will be wasting your time.

As your child shows that she understands or can use the signs, keep one step ahead by introducing three or four more, again choosing signs which are most relevant to her.

UNDERSTANDING THE MEANING OF WORDS

When children do not speak, parents often focus on getting them to talk by asking them to name things and copy sounds. It is more important for parents to focus on increasing their child's understanding of language since understanding is the key to speech.

- In daily life reduce your language to very simple words as described in General Guidelines, pp.89–90. Do not be tempted to fill in silences with waffle. Repeat everything over and over again. It may be very tedious for you but your child needs to hear a word repeatedly before she makes the connection between the word and the object, place or concept.

- Talk about the 'here and now'. Children do not develop a sense of past and future for some time. Talk about objects and activities which have meaning for your child, not about abstract notions or space travel.

- Remember children get fed up with naming things when they are aware that the adults already know the answer. If you are labelling things, try to do so in context. Alternatively, make a game by putting objects in a bag and get your child to choose one without your seeing and tell you what it is.

- If your child expresses her needs non-verbally, by signing or pointing, always state what she has communicated in very simple language. 'You want a drink', 'That's milk', 'You want the video'.

- Give a running commentary on what you are doing with your child as you play and as you do everyday things like changing nappies and washing. Use very simple (but normal) language to aid her understanding.

- Create an album with clear photographs of your child's own toys and familiar objects like her teddy bear, favourite beaker, car, highchair, bath, pet, family and so on. Look through the album with your child naming the pictures. Try to have just two pictures on each page. Ask your child to point to a specific picture given a choice of two or three.

- If she finds such an album helpful, you could add in pictures of favourite activities, family members, foods and use it as a communication book, which she can take around with her to show people and request things or people by pointing even if she does not have the spoken language.

- Create a scrapbook with images your child likes, cut from magazines, newspapers and catalogues. If she likes particular types of objects like animals or vehicles choose those. Bought picture books can often be full of pictures which are of no interest to your child.

- Look at very simple picture books with your child. Initially pictures must be very clear and easily understood. Photographs are especially good (for example the 'What's That' series by Campbell Books). Point to and name each picture and ask your child to find a named picture given a choice of two or three. (If there are too many on a page cover some up.) Always start by asking her to select her favourite picture which you know she will select, and then build on her success.

- Use everyday events to expand knowledge. For instance you could take the theme 'getting dressed':
  ○ As you are dressing your child name the different items of clothing.
  ○ Together make a book of clothing pictures taken from magazines and catalogues.
  ○ Dress a teddy or doll.
  ○ Give opportunities to choose between two items. For example 'Which shirt do you want to wear?'
  ○ Ask 'Where is...?' questions.
  ○ Pretend to forget an article, or ask 'What do we need?'

- Ask very simple questions like 'Where's the ball?', 'Where's Mummy?' or make simple requests such as 'Give me the spoon', 'Give me teddy'. If she does not respond, you respond for her saying 'Here's the ball', 'There's Mummy' and 'I've got the spoon'.

- Be silly. Put socks on your ears and get your child to tell you where they go. Put your socks on her feet and try to get hers on yours!

- Body parts are some of the first words children learn and there are lots of games you can play. You could sing 'Round and round the garden', 'This little piggy went to market', 'Head, shoulders, knees and toes'. Play tickling games naming the bits you are tickling. Name body parts in the bath – the most natural time. See Chapter 8, pp.196–197 for other ideas.

FIRST WORDS

There is nothing you can do to make a child say her first words. They will come if the child has the understanding, the ability to vocalize or sign and the opportunity. Concentrate on all the games listed in the sections 'Understanding that language means something' and 'Encouraging sounds'. It is by talking to your child and playing with her that you are most likely to help her language development. It also helps to introduce a few key signs from Makaton or Signalong.

EXPANDING INTO TWO-WORD PHRASES

A child has to understand two-word phrases before she will be able to use them. Once a child has a reasonable level of vocabulary, it is good to start combining words. Nouns are good for labelling things but speech therapists say that they are not actually very useful in terms of communication. Being able to say that something is a tree or a house won't get you very far. You really want to say something like 'red house', 'I want the house' or 'go into the house'. So it is important to concentrate on verbs (walk, run, sleep, eat, go, give) and prepositions (in, on, under). Adjectives (red, big, hot) come later.

It is important to know what 'understanding two words' means. It means understanding two 'information carrying' words. Therefore words like 'the' and 'a' don't count. In addition, a child has to demonstrate that she understands the words, and is not just picking up what is meant by the context. If you give a child a doll and a cup and tell her that the doll wants a drink and she gives the doll a drink, it does not demonstrate much because there is little else she could do. If, however, there is a comb, a drink, a doll and a teddy and she gives the doll a drink on request it would demonstrate two-word understanding.

- When your child is consistently saying single words, respond with a second. For instance if she says 'dog', respond by saying 'dog eating' or 'dog sleeping'. If she asks for 'more' ask her to say 'more carrot' or 'more milk'.

- To practise verbs comment on things you see around you, for instance 'dog running', 'bird flying', 'baby crying', 'cat sleeping' and 'car stopping'.

- Use two-word commands where your child has to show that she understands two words used together. 'Kiss granny' (when someone else is present as well) or 'Kick the ball' (where there are other objects around).

- Look at books and talk about what people, animals and things are doing.

- Use pictures of people doing things, for instance a man drinking, a woman driving and a child crying and ask your child to select the correct picture and to say what is happening.

- In everyday situations around the house expand your language into two-word phrases. Instead of just saying 'eating', 'drinking' or 'washing' say 'eating the bread', 'drinking the milk', 'washing my hands', 'brushing my hair'.

- Use dolls or teddies and everyday objects to mime activities which you can then talk about in two-word phrases. 'Dolly is eating', 'Teddy is sleeping', 'Dolly is reading'.

LEARNING ABSTRACT CONCEPTS

Children need lots of opportunities to generalize abstract concepts otherwise it is difficult for them to pick up their true meaning.

- Use every opportunity in your daily life to talk about abstract concepts like hot/cold, up/down, out/in, open/closed, high/low and heavy/light.

- Look at children's books which illustrate these concepts in different ways.

EXPANDING INTO THREE-WORD PHRASES

Children must demonstrate that they are understanding and using three different 'information carrying' words, not just picking up on context.

- When your child is consistently giving two-word phrases respond with a third word. For example 'Daddy gone' becomes 'Daddy's gone to work', 'Daddy's gone in the car' or 'Daddy's gone out'.

- Talk about the objects or activities your child is interested in. If she likes trains talk about the railway set and what is going on – trains, carriages, trucks, stations, drivers, passengers, going, stopping, pulling, up, down, through, bridges, tunnels etc.

- Do things with your child which will generate lots of talking. If you are shopping talk about what you are buying – its name, colour, size and what you will do with it. If you are gardening talk about digging, plants, flowers, colours, animals and birds.

- Read books together, talk about the pictures and the story.

- Play together – this is the main way children pick up language.

- Talk about everyday routines.

- At bed-time or bath-time or when Daddy or Mummy comes home, talk about things you have done during the day.

BEYOND THREE WORDS

If your child is using three words together she will probably continue to develop her language so that it gradually becomes more grammatically correct. Once a child is using three words she will be refining her grammar gradually. Further language development becomes more and more specific and is therefore beyond the scope of this book. However you can still encourage the use of more complex sentences by using the ideas listed above.

Parallel development

PROMOTING EARLY INTERACTIVE CONVERSATIONS

Dr Carolyn Smith is an educational psychologist on the Isle of Wight who has conducted research into early communication, based on the work of J. Bruner and others (Bruner 1983; Bruner 1990; Nadel and Camaioni 1993). She has devised the following approach[AQ], which emphasizes the need to return to the foundations of speech and communication, eye contact and turn-taking, because it is only once these are fully established that communication can proceed (Smith with Fluck 2001).

Play ideas

Watch your child at play and observe what she can do and likes doing on her own. It may be shaking a rattle, putting bricks in a container, drawing, playing with a doll or running a train along a track. It does not matter how simple it is because it is going to be the vehicle for language development.

Once you have decided what activity your child likes, take two identical or similar sets of toys so that you can mirror her. For instance, take two buckets with bricks and sit opposite and close to your child. Give one bucket to her and use one yourself. Copy exactly what she is doing. Mirror her but do not instruct her. You are trying to get her interest and thereby her co-operation.

Mirror what your child is doing

Your child will be intrigued and look at you to watch you copying her actions, thereby making eye contact. Repeat this as much as you can to extend eye contact.

You can start talking about what you are doing. Keep all language to a minimum to aid understanding, for example 'brick in', 'brick out' or 'brick on'.

This will lead to turn-taking. Your child will put a brick in the bucket then look at you and wait for you to copy her by putting a brick in the bucket. You do this, then look at her, and wait while she puts another brick in the bucket. You are taking turns – having a conversation.

Your child is learning that she can get you to copy her – she is learning to control you, which is a vital skill.

After you have been copying your child's actions you can start extending the game by doing something different and seeing if your child will copy you. As your child's understanding increases you can start using more complex language in your play.

Once her play with an adult is well established you can introduce another child in a structured setting, continuing the same ideas so that your child can learn to talk to and play appropriately with her peers.

PECS: PICTURE EXCHANGE COMMUNICATION SYSTEM

PECS is a system that was designed over 20 years ago to help children who find it difficult to initiate communication, make a request and get their needs met. It is most often used with children and adults with autism and communication difficulties and it relies on pictures (Frost and Bondy 1994).

Children learn to ask for something they want by presenting a picture of it to an adult. They can then go on through various phases of the scheme to make choices, respond to questions and make simple sentences. Initially, however, the objective is to get your child to request something using a picture. The key, often, is to identify the particular items, whether food, drinks, games or toys, which your child wants so much that she will be motivated to use the picture to request them.

Identify one item, say a particular toy which your child loves, then make a clear photograph or line drawing of it (depending on what is easiest for your child to understand). You have to ensure that she presents the picture to the adult in exchange for the toy. Initially two adults are needed to introduce the system: one to physically prompt the child from behind to give the picture and the other to receive the picture and immediately hand over the toy. As the exchange is made, the giver names the item. This is then repeated at regular intervals until the child understands that if she presents the picture of a doll, she will immediately receive the doll itself. She will then be able to use the picture independently to get what she wants. Over time you can put yourself further away so your child will come to you to make a request.

Gradually more pictures are introduced. The pictures can be attached to a board in an accessible place or put in a file which the child can carry around with her to use in different places as she needs them. This system is very user friendly in the outside world because everyone can understand the pictures used.

PECS is a system based on behaviour, which allows children to learn through cause and effect that they can get their needs met by communicating through pictures. It is highly rewarding for the child as the pictures introduced are tailor-made to the individual child. It does not require the language skills of speaking or the motor skills of signing, but uses permanent visual prompts which is helpful to children with processing problems. It focuses on the initiation of communication, which is an important part of communication. The introduction of PECS can alleviate a lot of the frustration felt by children who find communication difficult and which otherwise might lead to challenging behaviour.

For more information on the suitability of PECS for your child, talk to a health professional.

MUSIC THERAPY

Music therapy aims to enable children and adults to use music as a means of communication and self-expression. Young children with special needs who have problems communicating, interacting and expressing themselves through language may be stimulated to respond by listening to and making music. Music therapists use music to arouse and engage the child and then to develop a relationship with her.

At a very simple level, set aside some time during the day to play with music. Try singing songs, clapping your hands to rhythms and encouraging your child to play with instruments like tambourines, drums and chime bars. Encourage your child to listen to the sounds you make. Try copying what she plays on the instruments in order to develop an idea of turn-taking. Also encourage her to vocalize or play an instrument to accompany songs and music (Streeter 1993).

Making music with your child in this way will encourage listening skills, turn-taking and vocalization, which help language skills.

Alternatively, or in addition, contact the British Society for Music Therapy (see Chapter 11, p.248) for names of music therapists in your area.

CHAPTER 5

Physical Development

The theory
What is physical development?

Included in this section are all aspects of controlling the body, its muscles and its movements. The chapter has been subdivided into development of gross motor skills, which includes all larger movements of the arms and legs, and development of fine motor skills, which includes the delicate movements of the hands and fingers.

Gross motor skills
Chronological development
THE NEWBORN BABY

When babies are born they are totally dependent on their parents for help to survive but they do have the following reflexes, some of which are vital for their survival while others are throwbacks to our past evolution:

- sucking and swallowing
- rooting for the mother's nipple
- grasping
- walking (if a newborn baby is supported in standing position on a firm surface he will make steps)

- startle or Moro (if a baby thinks he is going to be dropped he will throw his arms back with open hands and then slowly bring his arms back together with clenched fists).

Newborn babies have very little muscle control and have to be supported and held securely. However, in the first months and years of life, the brain develops its ability to control the muscles and thereby the movements of the body. With the exception of those with very tight tendons who may have problems with sitting and find it easier to stand than sit, children gain control over their bodies in the same order because their physical development is governed by two fundamental laws.

1. Development proceeds from top to bottom (cephalocaudal law). Children learn to control their necks, then their backs, their hips and finally their legs. This is reflected in the fact that babies' heads grow first and look out of proportion to their bodies.

2. Development proceeds from the inside to the outside (proximodistal law). This is reflected in the way hands and feet seem small compared to the rest of a baby's body. Also children learn to support themselves on their elbows before their hands and they kneel before they can stand.

Physical development comes from active play. A child kicking his legs is developing his muscles. Similarly every time a child attempts to lift his head he is strengthening his muscles and developing his ability to control his movements.

HEAD CONTROL
Newborn babies are not able to support their heads. They gradually develop their neck muscles so that they can support their heads and look around while their backs are supported in a sitting position or while being drawn up by their arms from the lying to the sitting position.

As the neck muscles and those at the top of the spine strengthen, babies become able to lift their heads up while lying on their tummies.

FOREARM AND EXTENDED ARM SUPPORT
While lying on their tummies, babies learn to raise their chests off the ground first by supporting themselves on their forearms with arms bent and then on their hands with their arms extended straight in front of them.

ROLLING OVER

Babies first roll from their sides to their backs and later from their backs to their tummies.

SITTING UP

When newborn babies are placed in a sitting position they collapse forward in a rounded heap with a curved back. As their back muscles strengthen they need less and less support either from adults supporting them or from cushions at the base of the spine. Eventually they can sit unaided without risk of falling over backwards or sideways. When they lose balance they know how to save themselves by propping (putting their hand down to the floor by their side).

Weight-bearing on forearms and extended arms

Then they learn to turn sideways to pick up toys as well as lean forwards and backwards without toppling over.

CRAWLING

Children strengthen their hips and legs through vigorous kicking, either of alternate legs or of both legs together. They then learn to move around using one of a variety of methods. Some children crawl in the conventional way on hands and knees; some bear crawl on hands and feet; some do commando crawling on their tummies; while others use bottom shuffling instead and never crawl.

Some parents feel that crawling is a rather pointless stage on the way to walking and try to hurry children to stand up and walk. However, crawling is in fact an important skill because it makes children bear weight through their arms, thus strengthening the shoulders, arms and hands. It is this which gives children the strength and control to be able to develop fine motor skills like drawing and writing later on.

Crawling

HIGH KNEELING

Children learn to kneel with their bodies straight to their knees, thus bearing weight through their hips. This is a step towards standing up because the muscles around the hips only develop through taking weight.

HIGH STRIDE KNEELING

While in the high kneeling position, children learn to place one foot flat on the ground, take their weight over this foot and then push themselves into a standing position.

STANDING

In order to stand up children need to be able to stretch out their hips and knees and have the muscle power and balance to bear weight. Children first stand while holding on to furniture or people for balance and support before they are able to stand on their own.

WALKING

Before walking independently children must be able to stand and bounce up and down flexing their knees. They learn to cruise, i.e. walk sideways around furniture before walking forwards, holding an adult's hands or pushing a trolley or piece of furniture. Gradually as strength and confidence increase they need less support until finally they can walk alone for a few steps.

Initially, children walk with their legs far apart and their arms high for balance. They are very unsteady, tripping and stumbling frequently, and find it difficult to stop, change direction or look down.

As children become more agile, their feet come closer together and point forwards rather than outwards and they have a more regular stride pattern. They are able to change direction, bend down to pick up things from the floor and carry objects as they walk. They learn to push and pull toys and to walk backwards.

CLIMBING UP AND DOWN STAIRS
Once they can crawl children soon start to climb up furniture and steps. They climb in the crawling position using their knees and hands. They then climb using their feet rather than their knees which they place on alternate steps. Eventually they stand up straight in an adult posture but need to hold on to a handrail or someone's hand for support. Initially they put both feet on each step before finally learning to put alternate feet on alternate steps.

Coming down stairs is more difficult than going up. Initially children either slide down on their tummies feet first or bump down on their bottoms. Eventually they take an upright posture and walk down, first holding the rail and placing two feet on each step and then putting alternate feet on alternate steps.

BALANCE
An improvement in balance underlies much of children's later physical development. Children learn to stand on one leg, hop, walk on a narrow beam or line and negotiate stepping stones.

RUNNING
The transition from walking to running happens quite gradually. Children speed up their walking over time until they are able to run. They are liable to trip and fall initially but they learn to move around skilfully, turn sharp corners, carry, pull or push objects as they go, speed up and slow down.

CATCHING, THROWING AND KICKING A BALL
Children learn to catch large balls when thrown gently into their arms by putting their arms out rigidly. They gradually learn to bend their arms and to catch smaller balls and from a greater distance.

Children learn to let a ball drop from their arms before being able to throw it. They improve their skills in terms of both the direction and strength of their aim.

Kicking begins with children walking into a ball and kicking it accidentally; then they learn to kick standing still and later on the run, balancing on one leg. First kicks are very gentle but gradually children gain strength and control.

JUMPING
Children start trying to jump by bending their knees but their feet do not actually leave the ground. They first jump on the spot and then learn to jump off objects such as low steps and logs before being able to do a series of jumps without falling over.

Fine motor skills
Chronological development
THE NEWBORN BABY
Newborn babies keep their hands closed tightly in the reflex grip.

GRASP AND RELEASE
After the first few weeks babies lose this reflex and have to practise until they have achieved the control to grasp objects again. Gripping something is a complex action requiring children to be able to control their arm and hand movements, turn their heads to see the object and focus their eyes on it.

Babies bring their hands in front of their eyes and examine them. They are learning the rudiments of hand–eye co-ordination. They play with their hands, working out what they can do and how to get them to the right place. Initially they bat at objects dangled in front of them such as rattles strung across a pram or a baby gym.

They then learn to grasp an object with their whole hand, then to pass it from hand to hand and then to bang two objects together. Children initially grasp objects from the side and later have the co-ordination to grasp them from the top.

They learn to let go of objects later. At first, children release objects against a hard surface like a table top, the floor or an adult's hand. They later learn to release them into space. They are then able to start placing and posting objects into large containers and as their skills develop they can place them into smaller boxes and tighter holes.

Once able to release objects they learn to start throwing them, at first indiscriminately and later with force and direction.

FINE GRASP

Children learn to manipulate and explore toys by handling them, banging them and turning them in all directions.

Their grip becomes more refined as, rather than using their whole hand, they use their thumb and forefinger in the 'pincer grip', thus enabling them to pick up small objects such as raisins, crumbs and pieces of string. This ability to handle small objects will continue to improve over time.

Because they are using their fingers independently, they start to point and prod at things with their forefinger and to tackle posting shapes, stacking bricks and beakers, threading beads onto a string and doing puzzles (inset formboards followed by jigsaws). To begin with, they need to use large equipment which is easy to handle and they will have limited success – for example, stacking only two or three large wooden bricks – but gradually they will be able to stack more and more blocks and of a smaller size.

USING TWO HANDS TOGETHER

Children learn to use both hands together to carry out an activity, for example holding a bowl while scooping food out or pouring from one jug into another.

TWISTING

Twisting and turning handles and bottle tops and drinking from a bottle or a cup requires wrist control. Children learn to drink from a cup or twist easy knobs quite early but take time to gain the strength to turn large and stiff knobs, the precision to twist small ones and the ability to slide catches.

UNDRESSING AND DRESSING

To undress is easier than to dress (though children do learn fairly early to help when being dressed by putting their arms into sleeves and legs into trousers). First, a child will pull off a hat or a bib, or pull off socks and booties and then shrug off a coat or cardigan. Pulling off pants and trousers follows, then jumpers and shirts. Fastenings, particularly buttons, will be the trickiest element.

Children usually start dressing by putting on easy hats, then cardigans and shirts, followed by pants, trousers and skirts. Socks, shoes and fastenings are the most difficult.

FEEDING

Children learn to hold a bottle or lidded cup and drink from it. They gradually become more skilful so that they can use an open cup or beaker without spilling the contents.

Children learn to finger feed themselves with biscuits and pieces of fruit and vegetables, then they learn to feed themselves with a spoon if it is loaded for them and placed conveniently. They then have to learn to scoop the food onto a spoon. This is much easier with foods that stick to the spoon like yoghurt, Weetabix, rice pudding and semolina rather than foods like pasta which just fall off.

Having mastered a spoon, the usual progression is to learn to stab with a fork, then to use a spoon and fork together before finally using a knife and fork (but this would only be developing at school age).

USE OF TOOLS

Children learn to use all sorts of different tools which are part of everyday living for adults but require considerable manual skill and dexterity. The usual progression is scooping with spoons and spades, stabbing with forks, cutting with knives, then pincer action with pegs, tongs and scissors.

USING A PENCIL

Children first grasp a pencil or crayon with their whole fist, then they grip it higher up before the grip changes so that they use fewer fingers and hold it further down. This grip later becomes refined into the adult grip using the thumb and two fingers.

Because drawing and writing are complex skills requiring an intellectual understanding of the marks made, this aspect is included in Chapter 3, pp.58–59.

Games and activities

Activities to support physical development are also divided into gross and fine motor skills for ease of reference and understanding.

Gross motor skills

Chronological development

If your child has a physical disability or wears splints or a special soft helmet at times, check with your physiotherapist or occupational therapist before attempting these activities.

Some children with special needs find any kind of exercise distressing at first and would much rather be left alone. So try making it fun with lots of physical contact between you and your child or make it secure and soothing with music and reassuring talking as you play.

Children who are sensation-impaired have to be watched. If they have no sensation on one side they may get into dangerous situations without being aware of it – they will not be alerted by the pain.

TUMMY TIME

Because of lifestyle changes, babies are being kept in car seats, buggies and rocking chairs for long periods. They are being made too comfortable when they really need time on the floor, on their tummies, so that they can develop their muscle tone and physical skills by rolling over, reaching out and moving around. If your child is hypotonic, i.e. has poor muscle tone, this is even more important. Try to ensure that you take your baby out of his comfy car seat and find lots of opportunities to place him on the floor, on his tummy with toys to reach for.

Because of current advice on cot deaths parents are often unwilling to place their children on their tummies during the day, but this position is not dangerous for play and is vital for development – just make sure he is supervised.

POSITIONS

If you have a baby or a child who is not able to move, make sure that you place him in different positions during the day even if it is only for a short time. Don't always put him in his bouncy cradle or flat on his back in a cot or pram. Each different position encourages a child to use different muscles and see the world in different ways. Try some of the following:

- Place your child on his tummy on a mat on the floor.
- Place your child on his tummy with a rolled up towel under his chest.

Place your child in different positions

- Lay your child on his side – a particularly good position for playing with toys using both hands together.
- Place your child on his back flat on a mat on the floor.
- Sit on the floor with your legs stretched out in a V shape and place your child on his tummy over your leg either so that he is in a crawling position with weight through his legs and arms or so that his chest is raised off the ground.
- Sit on the floor with your legs outstretched and sit your baby close to you, between your legs, and supported by your body, and looking away from you.
- Sit on the floor with your legs bent and soles of your feet together. Sit your child on the floor, in front of your feet and looking at you. Support him as necessary either with his hands or by his hips.
- Kneel on the floor with your knees apart and sit your child between your legs looking away from you. You can support him by gripping him with your legs.
- Sit on the floor with your legs stretched out in a V shape and sit your child astride your thigh looking at you. This is a particularly good position if your child wants to push up to standing position.
- Lie on your back and place your child on his tummy on your chest. This is a good position for making eye contact.
- Also try carrying your child in different positions when you move around the house.

HEAD AND NECK CONTROL

When your child is lying on his back, cradle his shoulders and gradually draw him up into sitting position. Talk to him and make eye contact as you play.

It is also important to do this in reverse, gently getting him to lie back from sitting position.

Lay your child on his tummy and place a rolled up towel under his chest

WEIGHT-BEARING ON FOREARMS

- Place your child on his tummy on a mat on the floor. A firm surface is best, rather than a soft one like a carrycot. Try different surfaces to make it more interesting, for example, carpet, play mats, rugs, sheepskin, wooden floor or lino.

- Lay him on his tummy and place a rolled up towel or blanket under his chest so that he lifts his head and shoulders off the ground. This will give him a wider field of vision which he may well enjoy. Alternatively give him some toys to play with when in this position.

- Lie on the floor and place him on his tummy on your chest. Then encourage him to raise his head and look at your face.

WEIGHT-BEARING ON EXTENDED ARMS

- Place your child on his tummy with a rolled up blanket or towel under his chest so that his weight is on his elbows. Encourage him to reach for toys like a baby gym with one hand and then the other so that he takes the weight through his arms in turn.

- Lie on the floor on your back and place your child on his tummy on your chest. Use your body to get your child to shift his weight from one arm to the other.

ROLLING OVER

- Lay your child on his back and place one arm above his head out of the way. Gently push the other hip and leg forwards and use a toy as an enticement to get him to roll himself over onto his tummy. Do the same thing on the other side.

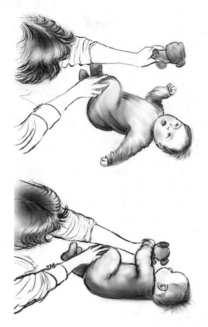

Encouraging your child to roll over

- Roll him half way and encourage him to continue the roll by placing a favourite toy to one side as an incentive.
- Place him on a rug or pillow and use it to gently rock him from side to side.

SITTING

- In order to help a child to sit up you need to practise the gradual pulling up and lowering described in the section on head and neck control (p.123) to strengthen all the head, neck and back muscles until he is able to sit alone.

- When he is able to support himself a little in a sitting position, sit him up on your lap and support him by holding his trunk and hips firmly. He will need less support over time.

Once a child can sit up he needs to develop his balance and strengthen the muscles in his torso so that he does not fall over at the slightest knock or movement. Instead he will be able to reach out to get things and prop (i.e. put his hand and arm out to touch the floor thereby save himself from falling over). Try the following ideas:

- When your child is sitting up, put things to his front and side to encourage him to reach out and grasp them and to maintain his balance at the same time.

- When he is sitting, gently rock him from side to side and from front to back so that he takes the weight on each side alternately.

- Sit your child astride your thigh, looking at you, and rock him sideways to improve his balance. This is particularly good if he has tight muscles around the hips.

- Sit him on a low stool or large firm cushion, hold on to his hips from behind and get him to reach forward for toys and objects.

- When in sitting position put his arms out to his sides, touching the floor and rock him so that he bears weight through his arms and stops himself falling over.

- Sing rowing rhymes with your child like 'Row row row your boat' and 'See-saw Margery Daw'. See Chapter 4, p.92, for the words. Sit on the floor with your child in front of you, hold hands and pretend to row backwards and forwards.

- Swings, rocking horses or other bouncy and rocking toys are all good exercises for strengthening the torso.

- Horse riding (through the Riding for the Disabled Association) is also extremely good for strengthening the body and for balance since every movement of the horse encourages the child to make a compensatory movement. It is particularly good for children who have tight muscles since they have to open up their hips on a horse.

- If muscle tightness is a problem, encourage your child to sit in a cross-legged position and not in the W position where he sits between splayed legs. This is also a good idea if he has a tendency to roll in on his ankles.

CRAWLING

Crawling is a very important skill to learn as bearing weight through shoulders and arms is vital for later skills using hands and arms. Parents are often anxious to move children on to walking as early as possible, but in fact children should be allowed to move on in their own good time.

It is important that children learn four-point or reciprocal crawling where they move one leg and the opposite arm together, rather than bunny crawling, in which they bring both legs up together.

- Hold your child on his front, supporting his tummy and fly him through the air. This will extend his back.

- Place your child, tummy down, over an inflatable roll with his hands and knees touching the floor. Then rock him backwards and forwards so he takes the weight alternately through his arms and hips.

- Place your child in crawling position and rock him backwards and forwards in order to give him the idea of crawling and to get him to start taking some of his weight on his arms and knees.

- Pass a towel under your child's tummy and chest and then hold it firmly above him. You can then lift his torso off the ground, while leaving his arms and legs in contact with the floor and get him to simulate crawling while you support his weight.

- Children often learn to crawl backwards before going forwards. Once your child is crawling backwards you can be confident that he will eventually move forwards. However, if you want to help him, place him on all fours with his feet against a hard surface – the sofa, wall or your hands – and encourage him to move forwards.

- When he is in the crawling position tempt him forwards with favourite toys placed just out of reach. Be careful not to make him too frustrated.

- Once crawling give him lots of practice by playing chasing games round the house.

HIGH KNEELING
Before trying to get your child to stand get him to balance on his knees. It will be much easier for him to bear weight through half the length of his legs than the whole length and it will strengthen and develop his hips.

- Place him in an upright kneeling position against a low table or a sofa on which there are toys to play with.

High kneeling position

- When he is in kneeling position push him gently from side to side so that he has to regain his balance.

HIGH STRIDE KNEELING
From the high kneeling position place one of his feet flat on the ground and draw him up with all his weight over his foot.

STANDING

- Kneel on the floor facing a chair or sofa. Sit your child on your knees facing away from you and with his feet flat on the floor. Rise up, raising your bottom off your ankles, and thereby lift your child into the standing position supporting him around the pelvis.
- Fix bars, for instance the side of an old cot, to a wall and attach interesting toys to encourage your child to pull himself up to standing using the bars.

- Cut the legs down on a small chair so that your child can place his feet flat on the ground when sitting down. Place the chair in front of some bars on a wall and encourage him to stand up.

- Holding your child's hands get him to stand up from a squatting position and then return again. This will help strengthen his leg muscles.

- Put toys on a sofa or low table and stand your child against it either with you behind him to give support or alone if he can support himself and encourage your child to play while standing. Some children will need to use a standing frame to do this (provided by physiotherapists).

- When he is in standing position, push him gently so that he is forced to regain his balance.

- Stand your child against a wall or in a corner and play a game with him, for instance banging a tambourine or playing with a ball.

CRUISING
Once he is able to stand try to get your child to cruise around the furniture using appropriate enticements like favourite toys. Create an environment where chairs, sofas and low tables are placed close enough for him to cruise easily.

WALKING
Don't be tempted to force your child to walk before he is ready. Remember that time spent playing on the floor and in the crawling phase is really important for shoulder and hip development later.

- When your child is standing against the furniture, lift one of his legs off the ground to encourage weight-bearing on the other leg.

- Once he is cruising, any kind of sturdy truck or trolley to push around will help him get the idea of putting one foot in front of the other.

- While your child is learning to walk it is important that he is supported from the front and at his hand height. Being hauled along from behind, gripped under the armpits, gives the wrong posture.

- Baby-walkers are not recommended by physiotherapists because they do not actually reproduce the walking motion. Children are supported in them and paddle their legs.

- Place your child on a push-along toy like a small tricycle or a car and push him round the garden. This is good for giving him the opportunity to push through his legs and gives the idea of movement.

- Place your child with his back to a wall and get him to hold an object which you also hold. Then encourage him to walk forward. A hoop is perfect for this since your child can hold the back and you the front.

BALANCE

Once a child has learnt to walk further physical development is generally reliant on a good sense of balance.

- Put your child in a large cardboard box and drag him around the room so that he has to balance as he is moved about.

- Get your child to step over small obstacles like a low wall made out of bricks, a plank of wood, door thresholds, a rope or sticks.

- Get your child to walk on uneven ground, up a slope, along a narrow beam, a low wall, a plank of wood or a thick line that you have drawn on the ground.

- Build stepping stones from bricks, upturned terracotta flower pots, slabs, mats or paint pots and get your child to walk on them.

- Get your child to stand on one leg.

- Encourage your child to use a scooter.

- When you are in the baby pool or shallow end of a swimming pool where he can stand upright, get your child to do different things. For example get him to walk, run, throw a ball, pour water or play with floats. He will have to work hard in the water to maintain his balance.

- Play throwing games; for example. throw a ball with your child, get him to throw a bean bag into a box or bucket or play skittles together. Throwing a ball affects balance and a child has to learn to compensate in order not to fall over.

- Play any racquet games where your child has to get to the ball and balance as he hits it with his racquet.
- Try kicking games; for example, kick a ball between you and your child and get him to try to score a goal or dribble round obstacles. This requires a good sense of balance as your child has to balance on one leg and kick with the other.

AGILITY

- Play hide and seek games.
- Play chase or 'it' games.
- Get him to play on equipment in playgrounds or at a children's gym session.
- Encourage your child to do somersaults, where there is a soft landing. But check with your physiotherapist first.
- Create your own playgrounds inside and outside. If you allow it, turn your sitting room into a soft play area for an afternoon, where children can climb over sofas, crawl through tunnels, jump off low tables, do somersaults on cushions, climb into boxes and crawl under chairs.

FLEXIBILITY

- In the swimming pool support your child when he is lying on his back and get him to kick his legs. This is good for flexibility in the legs and hips.
- Play hopscotch and other skipping and hopping games.
- Play 'Simon Says' and 'Here we go round the mulberry bush'. This is a good way of practising physical skills like stretching, bending and turning in a non-confrontational way. For example you can say 'This is the way we touch our toes' or 'Simon says stretch up high'.

CORE STABILITY

There is increasing awareness of the importance of developing the tone of the body's underlying core muscles around the trunk, hips and shoulders. As well as the ideas listed above for balance you could try the following ideas.

- Get your child to reach up for objects or to post letters.
- Get your child to stand on a large sofa cushion on the floor so he is a little wobbly and reach out for toys.
- Suspend a balloon from the ceiling and, supporting your child gently at the waist, get him to reach out and bat it to and fro.
- In the park, go on swings, rockers and chain bridges.
- Get your child to lie down on his back, with his feet flat on the floor and his knees up. Get him to lift his tummy up so you can roll a ball or send a train through the tunnel.

JUMPING

- Get your child to jump on a trampoline. A small one with a handle for him to hold as he bounces is particularly suitable.
- Encourage your child to jump off a step or, if swimming, off the side into the pool with an adult ready to catch him. You could use the Humpty Dumpty rhyme as a prompt. Encourage your child to bend his knees.
- Find low steps, such as the bottom step of a flight of stairs, logs or low walls, for your child to jump off.

RUNNING

Running comes gradually as children gain the confidence to speed up their walking. Give your child lots of opportunities to run around outside in a safe environment and, in particular, play chasing games to encourage him to speed up.

CLIMBING UP AND DOWN

Children start climbing soon after they start crawling. Start with low, easy climbs – onto a low stool or sofa. Use a favourite toy as motivation.

To show your child how to climb off a sofa or bed safely, place him on his tummy, get him to slide down backwards moving his legs and arms in sequence. This will show him how to get down feet first.

SPATIAL AWARENESS

Children need to learn where they are and where their limbs are in relation to other objects and the ground. By learning spatial awareness they learn how to move around objects safely without colliding into them, and when it is safe to jump off something high up.

- Provide opportunities to climb through, over and under objects for example tunnels, stiles, tables, large boxes and chairs. Play hide and seek games and encourage your child to hide in narrow, confined spaces. Soft play areas and playgrounds with climbing frames are good for this.

- Play with hoops as they are extremely useful for learning about spatial awareness. Put one over your child's head, get him to climb through it or draw it over him.

- Label spatial terms as you play – top of the slide, under the chair or through the hoop.

- Play games which encourage an awareness of body image. For example ask your child to become as small as a mouse, as big as a house, make a star shape, etc.

- Swimming provides an opportunity for your child to feel where his body and limbs are in the water.

- Horse riding, through the Riding for the Disabled Association, helps develop spatial awareness because it places children in a different position to normal. They have to be aware of the position of their limbs and where they are in relation to the ground.

RHYTHM

Children need to gain a natural rhythm to their movements and good co-ordination. Moving and performing actions to music is very helpful.

- Clap and sway to music with different beats.

- Listen to music and move appropriately; for example, march, gallop, creep and tip-toe.

- Dance to music of all kinds. If your child is not walking, you can encourage him to move to the music with his arms and torso or, if he is sitting down, to swing his legs freely in time to the music. Try all sorts of music from pop to jazz to classical.

FOOT–EYE CO-ORDINATION

Encourage your child to do the following activities which all improve foot–eye co-ordination:

- Kick a ball at targets using the left leg and then the right.
- Dribble a ball round obstacles.
- Run to the left, stop and then run to the right.
- Jump on the spot then to the left, the right, forwards and backwards.
- Hop on the left leg then the right leg.
- Play hopscotch and skipping.
- Do trampolining.
- Climb ladders.

Parallel development

PHYSICAL EXERCISE

It is important that children have lots of opportunities to practise different physical skills. Nowadays many young children are not doing enough exercise and their physical skills are suffering. Make sure your child has lots of opportunities to do exercise, especially if they have difficulties in this area.

PHYSICAL PLAY

Children should have a chance to experience lively physical play. You need to gauge what is appropriate for your child. Give him the chance to enjoy the sensation of movement but make sure he is feeling comfortable and confident by holding him securely and talking to him. Only take it as far as your child wants, never force it.

In addition, whatever your child's special needs, it is important not to be overprotective. Give him the opportunity to practise physical skills and thereby gain confidence. If your child's development is delayed, seeing him fall over may be alarming, since he is much bigger and has further to fall, but it is important that he has the chance to play. Playgrounds, soft play sessions, sand pits, beaches and gardens are good, relatively safe environments.

- Hold your child close to you and swing him round and round; tip him upside down and swing him by his ankles. Take your cue from your child and be as gentle or as rough as is appropriate.
- Dance to music while holding your child.

Dance to music holding your child

- Play roly poly by laying your child on the bed, holding him around the shoulders or by the hands and rocking him. Alternatively put his head and shoulders on a pillow and rock him with the pillow.

- Attend soft play sessions with bouncy castles, ball ponds and soft play equipment for children to climb up, down, under and over. Many recreation centres and private organizations run classes or sessions for young children.

- Attend gym courses for young children. In a safe and controlled environment children can learn to climb and jump and to experiment with simple gym equipment such as beams and trampolines.

RIDING FOR THE DISABLED

There are many Riding for the Disabled groups throughout the country as well as more specialist organizations which provide riding therapy for children with special needs (see Chapter 11, p.260).

Riding has two major benefits for children with special needs. First, it is extremely good exercise. If you don't ride you probably won't appreciate that the rider has to make compensatory movements constantly for the motion of the horse. It can also be used to encourage specific physical developments at every stage, for example strengthening the trunk, improving head control, establishing the prop reflex, replicating the walking motion, balance and spatial awareness. Second, interacting with horses can be very rewarding in emotional terms for children with special needs because it can offer a stimulating and joyful experience and perhaps provide a rare motivation. Riding also enables children who are not mobile to move around.

Riding

Usually a weekly riding session lasts for about 15–20 minutes. Children are led and side-walked by volunteers as considered necessary. The session typically involves different exercises and games on horseback.

SWIMMING

Swimming can be a wonderful activity for children with special needs, but only if the person who takes them is confident in the water. Your child will pick up on any nervousness and hesitancy on the part of the adult.

The main purpose of playing in a swimming pool at this age is to have fun. Any kind of playing, splashing, kicking and jumping in a pool is beneficial since it will improve muscle control and flexibility. In the water you have to work harder and yet you are supported. For children with a physical disability it can give a great sense of freedom and equality.

Be careful that your child does not get too cold in the water. Some children feel the cold more than others, especially if they are not very active in the pool. If, on the other hand, the water is very warm children may tire very quickly.

If your child is frightened of going in the water, introduce him very gradually. Begin perhaps by letting him watch from the side, then get him to sit on the side and splash, later get him to play with someone in the water perhaps with a ball or jugs. Only when he is ready should you bring him into the water properly. Sometimes it is worth approaching the pool from a different angle, perhaps by walking around the pool and going in from the other end. Many pools have attractive murals on the walls; use these as a distraction.

Swimming

Sometimes swimming pools can be very noisy, which can frighten children, so if possible choose a quiet time or attend a special session for people with disabilities; such sessions tend to be quieter than public sessions.

Some pools run water confidence courses for children from three months upwards. These show how to handle your child in the water and give ideas for games.

The following are ideas for things you can easily do in the swimming pool:

- Get your child to splash you with his legs and arms and make a big game of it by giggling, laughing, making silly faces and pretending to be upset to encourage him to do more. This is very good for strengthening muscles and for flexibility.

- Push a ball to and fro between you to strengthen his arms.

- Play jumping kangaroos. Hold your child's hands and get him to jump up and down in the water to strengthen his legs.

- Blow bubbles in the water. This is good for strengthening muscles in the throat and encouraging different sounds.

- Get your child to throw a ball to you; it will push him off balance and he will have to learn to correct himself.

- Hold your child and play 'Ring a ring o' roses', falling down in the water. You can go under water when your child is ready.

- Sit or stand your child on the side of the swimming pool, sing 'Humpty Dumpty' and get him to jump in.

Fine motor skills
Chronological development
POSITION

For all fine motor skills the position of the child is crucial. If he is badly positioned he will not be able to do many of the things described below. Always consider the position of your child (see Chapter 2, p.38). If your child has physical disabilities which make positioning difficult consult your occupational therapist for advice.

If your child has a visual impairment it is a good idea to keep toys in a box or on a tray so that he can find them with confidence.

ENCOURAGING USE OF HANDS

For children who have a problem with muscle control in their hands it is very important to encourage them to use their hands as much as possible so that they build up their muscle control and dexterity. The following games will encourage your child to open up his hand and use his fingers.

- Try playing with different substances and get your child to handle them in all sorts of ways – feeling, patting, poking, stroking and pulling.
- Play with sand both wet and dry or compost.
- Play with water (sometimes with bubbles, food colouring or fairy flakes).
- Play with play dough.

Play dough recipe

2 cups plain flour
2 cups water
1 cup salt
4 tbsp cream of tartar
4 tbsp oil
food colouring

Place all the ingredients in a saucepan and stir over a gentle heat until it reaches the right consistency. The play dough will keep for some time if kept in an airtight container in the fridge.

- Make up cornflour mixed with water. This has an amazing quality. It looks hard but feels soft and can be stretched into strings and different shapes.
- You can cook some extra spaghetti and let your child play with it when cold.
- Also try shaving foam and face cream especially those containing rough textured bits.
- Look at books which incorporate different textures and get your child to feel the surfaces.

- Get your child to mix cake dough and pastry with his hands.
- Play with the following materials: tin foil, bubble wrap, old newspapers and magazines, fabrics including carpet and furnishing material, soft balls, cotton wool and Koosh balls.
- Play with musical toys.
- Do some finger painting.
- Play splashing games in the bath or swimming pool.
- Do the 'Round and round the garden' rhyme. It will open up the palm of his hand.
- In a swimming pool get your child to push a ball to you on the surface of the water and keep it going to and fro between you.
- Put small sponges in the bath and get your child to pick them up and squeeze the water out.

BATTING

- Place light rattles in your child's hand or try wrist rattles or bells sewn on gloves to encourage him to move his hands.
- Place objects on a piece of string across a pram, cot, pushchair or bouncy cradle or use a baby gym. These keep toys within easy reach. They can be used if the child is able to sit or still lies on his back. Tie different toys on to give variety and change them regularly so he does not get bored. Try anything which is strongly coloured and likely to catch his eye, for example bells, shiny paper, pictures, rattles, mirrors, beads, unbreakable Christmas decorations and keys. Also try things which make a good noise. Even yoghurt pots and bottle tops make a good sound when tied together on a piece of string.

GRASPING

Play with:

- bean bags covered in a variety of textures and with different fillings like beans, buttons, pasta and coins
- soft blocks which are easy to grasp
- small rattles, teething rings and hoops

- pieces of dowel (a good size is 10 x 1.25cm (4 x 0.5in) diameter) covered in different textures such as silver foil, fur, velvet and bubble wrap.

PLACING AND RELEASING

- Get your child to release the object he is holding against a hard surface or your hands.
- Encourage your child to drop objects from a height so they make a nice bang. You could place a cake tin or box by his high chair and drop objects into it. Tie objects onto a piece of string so he can retrieve them and drop them again.
- Get him to place objects in a large shallow container, preferably one that makes a loud noise. Tins or small swing top plastic bins are good for this. Gradually reduce the size of the opening.
- Post objects like ping-pong balls in formula milk bottle tins by cutting a large hole in the top and making it smaller as your child progresses.
- Place a large object on top of another, for instance a toy car on an upturned cake tin, and knock it off noisily. To begin with use easily grasped, smallish objects placed on top of large ones. As your child progresses reduce the size of all the objects. For example use wooden, plastic or soft bricks to build towers.
- Get him to transfer objects from one container to another.
- Throw and roll balls to your child and encourage him to return them.
- Place bean bags into a hoop, balls into a bucket or other objects into a box or basket.
- Get your child to feed himself with pieces of fruit, vegetables, toast, crisps or biscuits.
- Encourage your child to help you tidy up toys and place them in the correct box.

POINTING

Having strength in the index finger is important for fine motor skills, in particular writing.

- Get your child to play with piano keyboards, press doorbells or switches.
- Point out pictures in a book. Ask 'Where's the bicycle?' type questions and get your child to point to the picture. Also point to people in photographs.
- Look at noisy books where your child has to press a button to hear the sound.
- Play with any toys with buttons to press, for example pop-up type toys, cash registers, press and go cars and tape recorders.
- Do finger painting with your child.
- Get him to dial using an old-fashioned dial phone.
- Encourage him to pop bubbles with one finger.
- Get him to draw on steamy windows or in wet and dry sand.
- Play with play dough or pastry when cooking and get your child to poke his finger into the dough to make holes.
- Play at flicking marbles and ping-pong balls.
- Play with finger puppets.

Dan likes putting his finger in my mouth. As a game I close my mouth suddenly and catch his finger before he can take it away. It's good for his eye contact too.

FINE GRASP

As a general rule start with light objects that easily fit in the hand and then gradually introduce heavier, smaller and larger ones.

- Play at building towers with bricks, beakers, household objects, Duplo, coins and buttons.
- Get your child to place things like Duplo, cotton reels, bricks and buttons in boxes and containers.
- Draw and cut out pictures of small animals like ducks, fish or frogs and draw a pond on a piece of paper. Get your child to place the animals in the pond.
- Draw an outline shape of a car or a dog and get your child to place shiny stickers inside the shape. You can glue yarn to the outline to make a raised edge.

- Play with Fuzzy Felts and sticker books.
- Play posting games, for example:
  - Place shapes in a shape sorter. Whistling and noisy shape sorters are particularly popular. Make your own shape sorter with different shapes cut into the lid of a formula milk tin.
  - Run cars, balls or marbles down marble runs or old cardboard tubes (from cling film or wrapping paper).
  - Use everyday activities like posting letters in a letter box, putting tapes in a tape recorder, putting books on a bookshelf, plates in a plate rack, cutlery in a tray, money in a piggy bank, ticket machine or charity box.
- Do puzzles – inset form boards or conventional jigsaw puzzles. It is often very difficult to motivate children to do puzzles because they are not terribly interesting or rewarding so look out for pictures which might stimulate your child. Duplo or other pull apart toys may be more interesting. Alternatively, try fitting together train tracks.
- Get your child to put clothes pegs around the edge of a cardboard box or pinch off pieces of play dough or Blu Tack.
- Encourage him to pick up small pieces of food such as peas, raisins, dried fruit, crisps, Smarties, chocolate buttons and hundreds and thousands.
- Get him to thread large beads with a thick and stiff piece of cord (washing line is very good to begin with), then move onto smaller beads and buttons and flimsier cord and eventually a shoe lace.
- Get him to place tops on pens, bottles and jars.
- Play with wind-up toys.

TWISTING

Get your child to do the following:

- Twist bottle tops, jar lids, door handles, control knobs on children's tape recorders and pop-up toys with twisting knobs.
- Spin balls and tops.

- Turn over cards in memory games.

ENCOURAGING TWO-HANDEDNESS
Though most people have a preference for one hand, children have to have strength and control in both hands to do two-handed tasks. Encourage activities which require two hands and if your child has a weak side, play games to strengthen that.

- Start by getting your child to move an object from one hand to the other in order to pick up another toy. So give your child one toy and then another and rather than let him just drop the first, get him to transfer it to his other hand. For example, two drum beaters to bang on a drum, two bricks to bang together, a cup and then a spoon to put in.

- Offer a toy directly in front of your child so that he can use either hand to take it. If you are trying to encourage one hand specifically, offer the toy on that side of him.

- Play with water or sand using buckets, funnels, jugs, sieves and cups and encourage your child to pour from one to another.

Encourage two-handedness with water play

- Catch and throw a large ball, or roll a large ball between you when sitting on the floor.
- Use play dough – rolling with a rolling pin, or patting with two hands.

- Get your child to hold his bowl or plate with one hand while he feeds himself with the other.
- Play with pull apart toys like Duplo or Stickle Bricks.
- When cooking get your child to stir the bowl and hold it at the same time.
- Encourage your child to bath or feed dolls, later progressing to dressing them.
- Play musical instruments like the tambourine, finger cymbals or hand-held drum.
- Play with screwing toys from a tool set.
- Get your child to pull tops off bottles and pens and unscrew toothpaste tubes then put them back again.
- Encourage your child to clap, for example by clapping to music or by singing songs like 'Pat-a-cake', 'Wind the bobbin up' or 'Five fat sausages' see Chapter 3, p.63 and p.74 for words.
- Get your child to clap bubbles to pop them.
- Play at threading beads onto a lace.
- Encourage your child to tear paper into thin strips by holding the paper with one hand and tearing with the other.
- Make a toy unsteady so that your child has to hold it steady with one hand while playing with the other.

If your child has a specific weakness on one side:

- Put cot toys and bath toys on the weaker side.
- Place a fork and spoon in each hand even if your child tends to feed with one.
- Place or offer toys to his weaker side to encourage him to pick them up and play with them with the weaker hand or at least pass them across to his stronger hand.
- Give your child a malleable substance like a soft ball, cotton wool or play dough to manipulate in the weaker hand.
- Put a sock or mitten over the stronger hand and encourage your child to pull it off with the weaker hand.

SHOULDER STRENGTHENING TO AID HAND CONTROL
Weight-bearing through the shoulders and hands is very important because you need strength and control in your shoulders and arms before you can attempt delicate movements with your hands.

- Play wheelbarrows with your child. If he cannot support himself on his arms alone support him under his hips.

- Encourage your child to crawl through tunnels and narrow places.

Crawling through tunnels strengthens the shoulders

- Get your child on all fours and then, while he maintains that position, play games that he enjoys like marbles, puzzles or card games.

- Get your child to kneel on all fours and stretch out his left leg and right arm and balance. Repeat using the opposite arm and leg.

- Get your child to do push-ups from his tummy.

TOOL USE
Pen control
Use crayons, pencils or pens which are easy for your child to hold. Chunky pens are better than thin ones and triangular shapes are good. Use ones which make good clear marks so that your child gets an instant reward for his effort and not ones which have to be held at a particular angle to work.

It is good to get children to work on an easel or wall because it makes them open up their wrist in a good writing position whereas if they are working on a flat surface they can keep their wrists very bent. Try chalking, painting, drawing, colouring or Fuzzy Felt games.

Try any games which encourage your child to enjoy making marks on paper or other surfaces, for example:

- make patterns in sand (wet and dry)
- put sand on coloured paper and move it around
- finger painting
- chalking.

For further ideas of games for writing and colouring see Chapter 3, pp.77–79.

Scooping

- Get your child to practise scooping with sand (both wet and dry).
- Allow him to use a spoon to transfer rice or pulses from one container to another.
- Get your child to scoop washing powder when you are loading the washing machine.
- Let your child dig in the garden or fill pots with soil.
- Try different cooking activities like dolloping spoonfuls of cake mixture into a tin or into individual pastry cases.

Pouring

- During water play or in the bath give your child lots of jugs, beakers, empty bottles, funnels and water mills so that he can practise pouring. Do the same with dry sand in a sand pit if you have one or in a bucket on a plastic sheet if you don't.
- Take turns watering flowers and pots with a watering can or jug.

Tongs

Use kitchen tongs to pick up objects (the movement is a useful preparation for using scissors because it requires a pincer grip).

Cutting with scissors

There are lots of different types of scissors to experiment with. Some are two-handed so that the parent can use the scissors behind the child to give the idea of squeezing and releasing. Others are called loop scissors and have a spring action so that the child only has to squeeze and not release.

You can borrow these from your portage home visitor, occupational therapist or playgroup to see if they help before you buy them, since they are only available from specialist suppliers.

- Get your child to practise using tongs first and to squeeze sponges because these require a similar movement.

- Start by giving your child light card rather than paper because this will be easier to cut. Cut long narrow strips so that he can cut across them and immediately see the strips cut in half. Gradually increase the width so that he has to make more and more snips.

- Draw thick lines for your child to cut along – initially straight lines, then with bends and then slight curves.

- Once your child can cut try different craft activities with him like cutting up pictures in magazines and old catalogues to make collages. Try cutting up old Christmas cards and birthday cards to make new ones, folding a piece of paper up and cutting holes to make snowflake pictures, and cutting and sticking coloured paper to make mosaics.

Using a fork

Get your child to stab food with a fork and practise this with play dough.

Cutting with a knife

Give your child a blunt knife to cut play dough into 'sausages'.

Parallel development

FEEDING

If your child is having problems feeding himself it is worth experimenting with different utensils. There is a wide range of cups, bowls and angled spoons and forks on the market. If this does not work ask your occupational therapist for advice and for the loan of more specialist equipment. Speech therapists will help with problems to do with muscle control such as chewing.

If you are working on improving feeding, don't try to do too much at once. Aim to improve feeding skills during one course of each meal and then let your child finger-feed the others. Alternatively, start off by taking time with the first half dozen mouthfuls and then allow your child to eat how he wants and gradually extend the time spent eating 'properly'.

Finger feeding
Give your child pieces of food such as breadsticks, biscuits, cooked vegetables and fruit which are easily chewed to establish the idea of taking food to the mouth.

Using a spoon
Load the spoon and get the child to take it to his mouth. Use the hand-over-hand method initially and then reduce the prompt as your child improves. Try an angled spoon to make it easier.

When he is taking the spoon to his mouth successfully, get him to replace the spoon in the bowl.

Scooping with a spoon for feeding
Move on to getting your child to scoop food onto his spoon.

- Start with food which is easy to scoop such as yoghurt, thick soups and stews rather than food which is likely to drop off a spoon, such as pasta.
- Play with your child at scooping with sand, water and other materials (see above under Scooping, p.147).
- Try placing a non-slip mat under the bowl or using a bowl with a suctioned bottom so that the bowl remains stuck to the table top and does not move around.
- Use bowls with near vertical sides rather than shallow ones with gradually sloping sides because they make it easier for the child to scoop.

Stabbing with a fork
Find opportunities for your child to use a fork, for example when eating food such as melon, pasta, cooked carrot, lumps of potato and meat.

Using a spoon and fork
Once your child can use a fork or a spoon introduce both together.

DRESSING AND UNDRESSING
Problems with dressing and undressing are often linked to a physical difficulty which is highly specific and which requires an approach geared to each individual child. In such a case you need to consult your occupational therapist. If, on the other hand, your child finds dressing difficult because of delayed or poor fine motor skills, rather than a specific physical disability, the following ideas may help.

Think of your child's position. Make him sit down to dress or undress. He will find it easier to concentrate on the process itself when he does not have to worry about supporting himself and keeping his balance as he moves around.

- Play dressing-up in adult clothes.
- Practise dressing during the day as a game when there is no time pressure. In the morning you are often in a hurry to get on and get out and in the evenings children are often tired and irritable.
- Break all skills down into small achievable tasks.
- Use backward and forward chaining techniques as described in Chapter 2, pp.40–41.
- Make up fastenings, for example zips, Velcro and buttons and stick them on boards which are solid and do not move around, then get your child to practise doing and undoing the fastenings.

HAND–EYE CO-ORDINATION
If a child has poor hand–eye co-ordination, use any or all of the above activities which practise fine motor skills. These will all assist progress in this area.

CHAPTER 6

Sensory Development

The theory

We all know the five senses of vision, hearing, touch, smell and taste, the most important aspects of which are covered in this chapter. But we may not be so aware of two further senses which we use all the time: the vestibular system (sense of movement) and proprioception (sense of body position). These are discussed further under 'Sensory Integration' since many children with special needs have problems in this area.

Vision

Vision is the most important of the senses in terms of development as it affects so much of how and what we learn. There is a strong interplay between vision and our ability to handle objects and to understand the world about us.

Newborn babies focus on faces more than anything else and specifically on those which are close to them, about 20–25cm (eight to ten inches) away, the distance between a baby and her parent when being fed. Given a range of different things to look at, a baby will choose a face. Babies are aware of vague shapes and dark and light and find patterns more interesting than solid areas.

Having learnt to focus on faces nearby, babies then learn to track objects, following them with their eyes as they move.

They then gradually develop the ability to see further and further away up to a couple of feet, to the other side of the room, and so on. Ultimately they have an adult range of vision.

Children use their sight to develop an understanding of object permanence, that people and things continue to exist even if they cannot be seen. This is covered in greater detail in Chapter 3, p.55, because it is crucial to children's understanding of the world and the way it works.

They then use their vision to gain an awareness of space, of where their bodies are in space and of how they can use what they see. For example, they learn that if they are sitting down and about to topple over, they can put their arms out to save themselves. They are thereby showing that they understand that the floor is a horizontal plane.

They also start to use their understanding of what they see in their interaction with other people. At a basic level they use it for eye contact, turn-taking and picking up on body language. Later they will use the information in their relations with others. For example if they see a toy at the other side of the room and someone else is nearby they ask that person to get it for them (Sheridan 1977; Sonksen 1983; Sonksen 1984; Sonksen and Levitt 1984).

Hearing

Babies' hearing and understanding of what they hear and where it comes from develops with age. Newborn babies are startled by sudden noises. They show this by responding to a loud noise with the Moro or startle reflex, throwing their arms back and widening their eyes.

They become interested in human voices and their mother's in particular. If they are content they will quieten, turn and listen to a voice talking or singing. If they are screaming for a feed, however, they are not likely to take much notice.

Children then start listening to all sorts of sounds, such as the vacuum cleaner whining or the tap running. They show excitement at certain sounds and sometimes will turn to sounds made close by. They also start to discriminate between the sounds they hear so that, for instance, they eventually recognize the noise made by the washing machine or a car engine.

Children then start to respond to the human voice with coos and gurgles, i.e. to take turns in 'conversations'. As they listen to sounds they try to work out where they are coming from. Usually they locate sounds with one ear before the other.

Gradually they get better at locating sounds. Initially they locate sounds made near them, for example a noisy rattle shaken nearby. Later they start to locate and recognize noises made further away within the room and then beyond, like a doorbell ringing and later an aeroplane flying overhead.

Children have to listen in order to process the sounds that they hear and understand that certain sounds are words and have meaning, i.e. that they are listening to speech.

We live in very noisy environments with a constant background of sound, such as the hum of traffic, birds singing, clocks ticking and washing machines whirring. Children therefore also have to learn to screen out all the irrelevant noises and focus on the important sounds like the person talking to them.

Children first hear high-frequency noises, which is why adults tend to talk to babies in high sing-songy voices and why babies respond better to women's voices. As their hearing develops they become able to hear lower frequencies too.

Taste

Children are born with a liking for sweet foods. In fact, breast milk tastes sweet. Children then acquire a taste for savoury foods as they are introduced to them. Children's tastes are largely established by the age of 15 months. So a child who has been only given sweet foods such as fruit purées will maintain a preference for them. It is important therefore that young children are exposed to as wide a variety of tastes and textures as possible at a young age.

Touch

Touch has an important place in providing comfort for babies. We swaddle and hold them to make them feel secure and loved. Babies also use their sense of touch to get information about objects and explore the whole environment. Another aspect is protective: they learn to move their hand away from a sharp blade or a hot pan or to save themselves from falling. Though children use their other senses to gain information, notably their vision, touch is still important. Think about how you extract a coin from your pocket or turn on the light in the dark. The way children use information from the tactile sense to adapt and modify what they do is the basis of their ability to plan and implement actions.

Touch is important in providing comfort

Smell

Babies use their sense of smell to find their mother's milk and they can distinguish between strong smells. As they get older they are able to distinguish further between a wide range of smells. Compared to many animals our sense of smell is under-used but it is an important factor in taste.

Sensory Integration

In addition to the well-recognized five senses of vision, hearing, taste, touch and smell, there are also two hidden, unconscious senses which are equally important.

- Sense of movement (the vestibular system). Receptors in the inner ear send messages to the brain to tell us where our body is in relation to gravity and the speed at which we are moving. They enable us to know when we are upside down doing a somersault, for example.

- Sense of body position (proprioception). Proprioceptors in our muscles and tendons tell us about our body position, for example that our hand is above our head, and the relative force we are using.

These two senses work closely with our sense of touch.

All the senses should work together subconsciously by sending messages to the brain where the information is processed, organized and used. This is called Sensory Integration. We might use the information to negotiate an obstacle course, find something in the dark or gauge the force needed to bang in a nail. The processing of different sensory information by the brain is vital to the development of gross and fine motor physical skills and good co-ordination. It also has a profound influence on aspects of our development which may not seem related to the senses. Our brain works out the meaning of sensation and how to respond which is then the basis for developing our understanding of our environment and our ability to control our bodies, feelings and attention. The interpretation of our sensory experiences affects our ability to respond appropriately to situations and to plan all types of activities (Cribbin et al. 2003).

Babies and very young children primarily use the information from their tactile, proprioception and vestibular senses to move, to explore and to learn.

Games and activities

Vision

GENERAL ADVICE FOR CHILDREN WITH VISUAL IMPAIRMENT

- Give your child a running commentary of what you are doing in simple language so she can understand what is going on.

- Use the same words for the same activities, to give warning of what is going to happen, and then develop the idea of language by association.

- Talk to your child gently before approaching to give her warning and to avoid startling or frightening her.

- Place toys on a tray so that your child can locate them and keep them contained. Once she is used to the position, move them around so she develops the idea of object permanence and improves her feeling skills.

- Use a baby gym so your child can touch toys without stretching.

ADVICE FOR CHILDREN WITH VISUAL PROCESSING PROBLEMS
Some children appear to have good vision (visual acuity) when using standard eye tests, but because their brains cannot process the visual

information received they have poor visual function in the real world. Eye tests show shapes and letters on a clear background with high contrast, which may be easily identified by a child. At the same time however she may not be able to make sense of crowded images. So, for example, she might be able to identify a shoe in clear space but perhaps not if it was placed in a pair or among other objects. With such children:

- make sure that pictures and objects have high contrast
- make sure there is space around objects
- allow the child to come closer to be able to see more clearly
- play games of finding an object amongst a number of different things on a tray or looking for things in a drawer or container
- use some of the ideas below for stimulating looking and tracking.

STIMULATING LOOKING
Children with a visual impairment usually have some vision and it is important that they learn to use well what vision they have. Therefore try to stimulate what vision there is as much as possible. Children with special needs other than a visual impairment may also need encouragement to look at things and reach for them.

The RNIB (Royal National Institute for the Blind) advises parents of children with visual impairment:

- Big toys are best – fiddly little toys are difficult to see and handle.
- Colourful toys are easier to see – eyes work on contrasts so start with black and white then move on to colours like red and yellow. Fluorescent colours are also good as is shiny and holographic paper.
- A bright well-lit environment is best.

(RNIB and Play Matters/NATLL 1987)

Use visually exciting materials
Newborn and young babies can only see a very short distance so any pictures or objects must be placed very close to the baby, about 25 centimetres (ten inches) away initially. Mobiles, however colourful, will not be seen unless they are really close to the child.

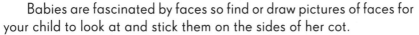

Babies are fascinated by faces so find or draw pictures of faces for your child to look at and stick them on the sides of her cot.

The following are also likely to stimulate interest and encourage a child to look:

- glittery, shiny, silver or holographic paper covering objects
- lights – torches shone round the room and on holographic paper, fairy lights, books and toys with flashing lights, fibre-optic torches available from joke shops and fun fairs
- shiny objects which catch and reflect light
- mirrors
- hard, shiny toys rather than soft, furry ones
- tactile toys with interesting textures to feel
- spare keys
- balloons
- metallic toy windmills
- musical toys.

Find an organization with a sensory room which your child could use. Sensory rooms are designed to provide maximum stimulation of the senses in a fun, educational or therapeutic way. They use music, textures, aromas but particularly lights – especially fibre-optics.

> I'll never forget when I took Natasha into the sensory room when she was six months old. She hadn't really responded to anything visually before, but I brought a 'spray' of fibre-optic lights towards her face and she suddenly startled back, as if she'd seen something for the first time. Well, that was it. We bought loads of fancy flashing torches and lights to stimulate her vision. I am sure it helped, because now she has learnt to use what little vision she has without the need for flashing lights.

Use other senses

Use activities which engage each of the other senses to encourage a child to look, such as the following.

Sound

- Hide squeaky toys.

- Sing and recite nursery rhymes with actions.
- Play with musical toys and instruments.
- Hang up wind-chimes around the house.

It is good to use noisy toys. If possible find toys with different sounds so that your child can recognize objects by the sound they make. If your child hears a noise, she needs to see or touch the source of it so that she learns the importance and meaning of sounds. If she does not she may learn to ignore sounds.

Touch

Gather objects from around the house for your child to play with. You could make a lucky dip bin. Children's toys seem to be predominantly primary-coloured plastic, yet children need to explore other weights, textures and qualities. Use candles, wooden spoons, saucepan lids, metal spoons, cardboard, Cellophane, tissue paper, inserts from chocolate boxes and biscuit tins, sponges or fabrics (silk, fur, sequins, leather, carpet, sandpaper or furnishing fabrics).

Taste

All children explore with their mouths because it is the most sensitive part of the body.

Smell

Mix very small amounts of safe aromatherapy oils, such as lavender or chamomile, with cream and spread some on her hands and feet. Exaggerate the act of smelling them and bring them to her nose. Also use horrible smells like onion.

TRACKING OBJECTS

- Attach a balloon to a piece of string, pin it to a door frame or the ceiling and bat it for your child to follow with her eyes.
- Push friction cars so that they move slowly across the floor; ones with flashing lights or moving parts are particularly good.
- Roll a ball in front of your child. Use a brightly coloured one with a bell inside, or one that flashes as it moves.
- Move a squeaky toy across your child's field of vision and get her to follow it with her eyes.

Tracking an object

- When your child is in her highchair move a toy around the outside edge of the tray so that she follows it with her eyes.
- Get your child to throw a soft ball at a target on the wall, in a net or a box.
- Use fluorescent materials in a darkened room.

Hearing

GENERAL GUIDELINES

When talking to your child, make sure you are near her and in front of her. Get her attention, make sure she can see your face and make eye contact. Turn off music, radios and TVs. This is particularly important if your child has a hearing impairment.

ENCOURAGING LISTENING

- Focus on the noises that things make.
- When looking at books or playing with toys, ask 'What noise does the cow make? Moo'. Talk about the dog, car, bicycle, aeroplane etc.
- Play with noisy toys with different beeps, bells and sounds. It is also quite easy to fill plastic bottles and containers with different things to make different sounds – rice, pasta, beans, buttons, water etc.

- Go round the house listening to the noises made by different household objects like the fridge, washing machine, doorbell, vacuum cleaner, taps and clock.

- Go on listening walks. Outside the house point out noises such as the birds, the rustle of leaves, rain, fountains and traffic.

Go on listening walks

- There are games available where you match pictures to sounds on a tape. Alternatively, you can make your own up by recording noises around the house (washing machine, dog, clock, blender, doorbell) or in the vicinity (cars, rain, birdsong) and you can take your own photographs to go with them.

- Play listening lotto. Each of you should have a lotto board. Make a pile of the individual cards and say what each picture shows, get your child to call out if it is on her board. The first person to complete her board is the winner.

- 'Ready, steady, go' games encourage a child to listen for the all important signal to start.

LOCATING SOUNDS

- Talk to your child as you walk in and out of the room she is in to get her to pick up on where the sound is coming from.

- Hide a noisy toy under the tray of your child's highchair and get her to locate it.

- Play games to find a noisy toy, for instance hide a radio or clock which ticks loudly and get your child to find it. Alternatively you can hide any toy and then make louder noises as she gets nearer and quieter noises as she gets further away from it.

- Focus on the noises that you hear in the house or coming from outside and with your child try to find where they are coming from. For example listen out for and locate the washing machine, the doorbell, the coffee machine, the helicopter, etc.

MUSICAL GAMES
Musical activities are very good for listening and concentration and also for timing and anticipation. Try the following activities:

- Get your child to play with musical instruments such as drums, cymbals and mouth organs.

- Play an instrument and let her listen. It is great if you can play the piano, guitar or recorder well but children are equally fascinated by the sounds made by instruments which anyone can play such as drums, whistles, mouth organs and kazoos.

- Get your child to play a musical instrument as an accompaniment to your singing or a tape. Get her to stop as soon as the music stops by asking her to put her arms in the air.

- Clap, knee bounce, hum or sway to songs to encourage a feeling for rhythm.

- Perform action rhymes to encourage listening and concentration. For example:

  Miss Polly had a dolly who was sick sick sick
  So she phoned for the doctor to come quick quick quick
  The doctor came with his bag and his hat
  And he rapped on the door with a rat-a-tat-tat.
  He looked at the dolly and he shook his head
  He said to Miss Polly 'Put her straight to bed'
  Then he wrote on his paper for a pill pill pill
  'I'll be back in the morning yes I will will will'.

- Also use some of the songs with actions listed in Chapters 3 and 4. For example 'Wind the bobbin up' (p.63), 'The wheels on the bus' (p.63), 'Here we go round the mulberry bush' (p.63), 'I'm a little teapot' (pp.63–64), 'Ring a ring o' roses' (p.95) and 'Five currant buns in the baker's shop' (p.75).

- If your child has a hearing impairment, get her to touch the speakers of a CD or cassette player (make sure it won't damage them) to feel the vibrations of the music and play games using the on/off button. Put her hand on a drum or tambourine while you bang it.

- Play musical bumps, mats, chairs or statues, where your child has to listen for the music to stop and then do something, for example stand still, sit on a chair, put a hat on or jump. Use fast and slow rhythms.

- Play different types of music and encourage your child to move appropriately, for example marching, galloping and tip-toeing.

- There are music and movement classes for pre-school children which use some of the ideas above. Alternatively, you could try to meet up with a few friends on a regular basis for short music sessions because it can be quite difficult to organize your own children for musical activities if you are on your own at home. Don't be embarrassed. Try singing nursery rhymes, playing musical instruments, playing some musical games and moving to music. Children love it.

Taste

Introduce your child to a wide variety of different tastes and textures of food. Even if she shows a preference for one particular taste, others should be introduced. Make sure you introduce savoury flavours and different textured food. If you are concerned that your child has food fads which make it difficult for her to have a balanced diet, seek professional advice.

Touch

To encourage your child to develop her sense of touch you could try the following ideas:

- messy play – use cornflour, sand, lentils, shaving foam, cooked spaghetti, uncooked rice, soap flakes or mud pies
- arts and crafts activities involving different textures such as finger painting, papier maché, modelling with clay, play dough or plasticine
- water play – add colours or bubble bath to make it more interesting
- cooking activities – particularly making pastry or bread
- gardening activities such as digging or filling pots with compost
- lucky dip – with different objects from round the house.

Playing with playdough

Babies gain sensory and emotional benefits from being touched and held. You could also consider using baby massage techniques either learnt from books or local classes.

Smell

We probably underestimate the power of this sense, which can be evocative and therapeutic. You could take the opportunity to incorporate different smells into your child's play. For example, you could try using aromatherapy oils in a burner, add food essences such as vanilla to water for water play or plant aromatic herbs and plants in the garden for her to touch and smell. Be aware that smells can trigger very strong emotions, particularly if they are associated with a bad experience in the past.

Sensory Integration

All children enjoy sensory experiences. Just think how much some children love going on swings and roundabouts at a park or running around madly. As well as giving pleasure, these experiences are important developmentally and children will find ways of getting the experiences they need. Make sure you give your child plenty of opportunities to indulge in sensory play and to have sensory experiences. Give your child access to a full range of sensory experiences in a safe, acceptable and appropriate way, such as:

- play in the garden or take trips to the playground for sliding, swinging, spinning, jumping, climbing and somersaults
- go trampolining and swimming
- have toys which are safe to mouth – teething toys, blowing toys such as whistles etc.
- encourage messy play – mud pies, finger painting, play dough, cooking, playing with cream or shaving foam on a tray
- play rough and tumble games – cuddles, tickles, massage, wrapping in blankets and rocking and rolling.

Some children have extreme reactions to certain sensory experiences which can interfere with their daily life. If you think your child has such a problem (called Sensory Integration Dysfunction), then ask a professional, most likely an occupational therapist (OT), to carry out an

Play rough and tumble games

assessment to work out your child's particular areas of difficulty. The OT will probably suggest ways of creating an appropriate environment to meet your child's sensory needs and may also offer individual therapy sessions depending on severity and provision.

Children can be hypersensitive (over-sensitive) to certain inputs in any of the sensory areas. Children who are particularly sensitive to touch are described as tactile defensive, or to loud noises as auditory defensive. They may hate loud noises, the texture of certain fabrics or particular foods and can react with a flight, fright or fight response to such sensations. Equally some children are hyposensitive (under-sensitive) to certain inputs and need extreme sensations such as spinning around madly, jumping off furniture or flashing lights in order to become responsive. Children often have a highly individual set of responses, being hypersensitive to certain inputs and having a normal or hyposensitve reaction to others. They can also fluctuate between the two. Try to work out which sensory activities she really enjoys (such as being held tightly, chewing toys or listening to loud music) and which ones she avoids (such as roundabouts, light touch, certain textures in clothes and loud bangs). It can, however, be difficult to pinpoint your child's particular sensitivities, so you may need help from a professional.

One day I picked up Christopher from his playgroup to be told that he had got rather anxious during the session. Apparently a helper had got the Hoover out and he had got rather agitated so it was put away because she thought he hated the noise. In fact he absolutely loves Hoovers and was probably only excited to see it and then distraught when it was removed.

It is important to appreciate that your child is not being naughty when she responds in an extreme way. She may run away because her brain cannot process the information it is receiving and she needs to escape or she may act inappropriately because she is desperate for a sensory experience which she needs. Alternatively she may be doing everything she can to avoid a sensory experience which she knows she cannot handle, for example by blocking out the sensation by some other action such as screaming or headbanging which she can control.

Try to work out where her sensitivities lie and to work within her limits. Her limitations need to be respected, tolerated and accommodated by everyone, so make sure that all carers and family members know her sensitivities and take the same approach. You first need to find a strategy to enable your child to cope and feel comfortable. Only then might you gradually be able to encourage her to extend her tolerance by very small degrees. This is a very complex area, so if you are finding it difficult then seek professional advice. For example, a child who does not like wearing clothes should be given only the lightest and softest of fabrics to wear – often secondhand clothes which have been washed many times are the easiest to tolerate. T-shirts and shorts might be the easiest to wear, then you could introduce trousers or long-sleeved T-shirts. You may need to cut labels out of her clothes or wash clothes in the same powder each time for the same scent.

If you have a child who cannot cope with noise, you could ensure that your house is quiet with no radio or TV but then perhaps start playing music for short periods. Some children might cope better with soft whale music or even-toned music played very quietly in the background. Then you could over time extend the period or increase the types and volume.

A child who is very sensitive (hypersensitive) to touch may not like light touch especially if it is unexpected, for example if someone were to touch her from behind. Always approach from the front, giving advance warning and use firm touch.

On the other hand, children who are hyposensitive need a lot of input for sensations to register and can enjoy extreme experiences. They will crave these sensory experiences and will probably find a way of achieving them, so it is important to find safe ways to facilitate them. For a child who likes jumping you could try a trampoline with a safety net, whilst swings and roundabouts are good for children who like spinning, or they may like rough and tumble games. Some children need to feel pressure on their bodies to feel secure and might find it helpful to wear a backpack or bumbag with something heavy inside and may need heavy blankets to sleep comfortably at night.

Some children find it helpful to wear a backpack

SELF-REGULATION

Consciously or unconsciously, we all use 'sensorimotor' strategies to control how we feel and to get ourselves into the right mental state for whatever we are doing. For example, if we want to concentrate in a meeting we might fiddle with our hair or suck a pencil or if we want to relax ready for bed we might have a milky drink or a bath. All of us find our own personal set of strategies that work for us. This is often referred to as a 'sensory diet'.

Children have to learn these strategies and young children with special needs will require help to regulate themselves (Williams and Schellenberger 1994). If not they may become more and more fired up when they should be calm, subdued when they should be alert and engaged, or veer madly between the two extremes.

We are probably very aware of the cognitive methods that we use to get ourselves or our children into the right frame of mind for an activity. We might use the promise of a reward, or set ourselves a target or give ourselves a motivational chat. However sometimes a better alternative is to do some 'heavy work' or proprioceptive input. This is a sensorimotor activity which generates resistance such as pushing, lifting, climbing or chewing. This 'heavy work' sends a strong message to the brain, thereby engaging the cerebellum and getting us into the right state of mind, either calming us down or gearing us up as needed so we can plan our actions and modify our behaviour. 'Heavy work' in one sensory area will benefit all sensory areas – so it does not matter which type of activity you do. You will probably find some ideas work better than others for your child. Observe her and the methods she uses to regulate – maybe rocking to music to calm down or jumping around to become alert.

'Heavy work' will benefit all sensory areas

Try to encourage her to do some of the following activities so that she can regulate her energy and alertness levels. The effect of heavy work only lasts for a matter of hours so these activities need to be built into the day at regular intervals. Try using these as a precursor to a difficult situation to get her into a coping state of mind rather than motivating her through a reward system. Maybe go to the park before the supermarket rather than afterwards.

My son loves tickles and will demand 'tickle me really really hard up there' at various times during the day. What he wants is actually very deep massage of his neck and shoulders and I do that for him several times each day. Amazingly it calms him down!

You could try:

- blowing toys – bubbles, musical instruments
- sucking – straws with a thick liquid

Using a straw to drink a milkshake to help self-regulation

- eating chewy or crunchy food
- wearing a bumbag or rucksack with something heavy inside
- rough play, cuddles, wrapping up in a blanket
- bouncing on trampolines
- putting sofa cushions on your child and sitting on them gently
- carrying heavy things – tidying toys or books up
- pushing wheelbarrows or pushchairs, putting chairs under the table, pushing a brick trolley with something heavy in it
- washing the floor, vacuuming, sweeping up

- playing with wet sand or in the garden – digging and filling up and carrying buckets
- having a dark space where the child can sit with bean bags or cushions on top of her
- climbing or crawling over obstacles
- wheelbarrow races
- playing with plasticine, play dough or Blu Tack.

CHAPTER 7

Social Development

The theory

What is social development?

Social development starts when a child gains awareness that he is a separate individual, distinct from his mother and other people, and has a concept of himself and his identity. Once he has understood his own individuality he can go on to learn the skills needed to live alongside others in a community – his immediate and extended family, friends, playgroup and the wider community of neighbours. Children have to learn to mix and communicate with others, to share things and take turns and to live by the generally accepted rules which govern each community.

Chronological development

THE NEWBORN BABY

As soon as a baby is born he is a social animal. He does not want to be left alone, but finds comfort and security in being held and cuddled by other people, especially his mother. He cries to get attention and in order to have his needs met.

INTEREST IN PEOPLE

Newborn babies are programmed to find the human face the most interesting object of attention. Quite quickly, and even with the limited vision of a newborn, they study faces, either real ones or representations, and make eye contact.

Babies then usually learn to smile within weeks. Smiling has a powerful and positive impact on carers and babies get the instant reward of more attention. It is very difficult for parents to resist their baby's smile. Coos and gurgles have the same effect, binding parents closer to their baby. Babies are also learning a vital lesson. They are discovering that by smiling and making noises they can use adults to get what they need. They are also learning, at a very early stage, that people are important: this is vital because it is through other people that they will learn about themselves, about what they can do and about the world around them.

ANTICIPATION OF FAMILIAR ACTIVITIES
Your baby will start to become aware of familiar activities and will begin to recognize visual and sound clues which tell him what is about to happen. He learns to recognize that the sound of the bath tap running means that he is going to have a bath, or that his coat and boots appearing mean that he is going to go out. Parents recognize that their child is picking up on the 'cues of life' by signs of anticipation and excitement. Some children will start kicking and squeaking excitedly when their clothes are removed in anticipation of having a bath. It may seem obvious but anticipating familiar situations and routines is actually a very important skill without which we would not be able to make sense of our environment. This is the basis for our own feeling of control over our lives.

CONCEPT OF SELF-IDENTITY
A child gradually gains a sense that he is an individual with a separate identity to his mother. He does this by learning about his own body, what it can do and how it feels. He learns that he can control his own limbs but not those of other people, that if he chews his feet he can feel it but not if he is chewing his father's fingers. At around the same time children learn that objects and people continue to exist even when they cannot be seen (object permanence – see Chapter 3, p.55). A baby will scream when his mother leaves the room because as far as he is concerned she no longer exists. It is only later that he understands that she continues to exist, although she cannot be seen, and will return.

TURN-TAKING
Turn-taking skills are most easily observed when a parent talks to his or her child. For example, a father says something to his child who then

responds with noises and then stops and waits for a response from his father before making further noises. This can continue until there has been an extended 'conversation'. Turn-taking is fundamental to communication and language skills and is therefore fully described in Chapter 4, p.84, but it is also crucial to social development since concepts of turn-taking, sharing and consideration for other people are the basis of social skills.

GETTING ADULT ATTENTION
Newborn babies cry to get attention and then leave their parents to go through the routine of checking whether they want milk, a nappy change, sleep, winding or a cuddle. Parents soon learn to recognize different cries for hunger, pain, tiredness or boredom. Later on, children learn to use more sophisticated methods to communicate. They make different sounds and noises in different situations. These are not words but they are an important precursor to speech and demonstrate that the child is seeking to interact with other people.

An early example of this is when a child wakes up in his cot and starts shouting rather than crying to show that he is awake and wants his parents to come and get him. Another example is when a mother is playing with her child, the child will use smiles and gurgles to keep her interest and stop her going off to do something else.

A child has to learn that he can affect, influence and manipulate people around him. He has to see the point of social interaction, in other words that he can get adults to do things which he cannot do by himself. If parents are uninterested in their child and do not respond to him appropriately, the child will lose interest in social interaction with a detrimental effect on all his development.

These early stages of interaction may lay the foundation for later behavioural problems. A child who gets lots of attention for playing nicely will, one hopes, continue in that vein, whereas a child who is ignored unless he makes a fuss may continue to use bad behaviour to gain attention in the future.

RECOGNITION OF FAMILIAR PEOPLE AND FEAR OF STRANGERS
Newborn babies recognize their parents very quickly by their smell and the sound of their voices, which will have grown familiar during pregnancy. Initially babies are not frightened of strangers and can be passed around family and friends without difficulty. However, later on they start to recognize familiar people, family, friends and relatives

and, as a consequence, in self-preservation, become shy or frightened of strangers. As they gain experience and confidence that adults will not harm them, this fear of strangers diminishes.

CO-OPERATING AND COPYING
When children are learning early physical skills, such as sitting up, walking and placing objects, they are largely self-absorbed, experimenting by themselves. They tolerate some interventions from adults and go to an adult for needs like food and comfort.

Next, they start to co-operate with adults in play such as 'pat-a-cake' and by obeying simple commands such as 'come here' or 'give me the cup'. They help adults in play, for example with feeding a doll or rolling a ball.

At the same time, they begin to copy what adults are doing, often housework activities such as wiping a table, sweeping the floor or dusting. They also start to copy gestures such as waving goodbye or saying 'sshh'. Children learn to fit into society by copying the manners and behaviours of those around them.

SHARING AND TURN-TAKING
As children understand object permanence, see Chapter 3, p.55, and as they have a concept of themselves as separate individuals, they become possessive about their belongings and toys and are reluctant to give them up to another person or child or to leave them. Equally, they have no concept of sharing the attention of an adult, for example wanting books read exclusively for them and not for their siblings or friends. Gradually the ability to share possessions and take turns in activities comes as they see that they themselves will ultimately benefit. They realize that if they give up their toys to other children now they will get them back later and others will be expected to do the same for them.

TESTING THE BOUNDARIES
When children learn enough self-awareness, they start to have their own desires which don't always coincide with those of their parents. Initially they can easily be distracted with a different activity. For instance, if a child wants a particular toy which someone else is using he may get cross, but will easily be placated with another equally interesting toy.

Later on, children are more determined and not so easily distracted so they may start having tantrums if thwarted. They need to know the rules and the boundaries of acceptable behaviour. They like to test the boundaries to see if they can be moved. Once they discover the limits cannot be moved they feel safe and settle down to operate within the acceptable boundaries. If they learn what these rules are, they come out of the period of tantrums much more amenable and affectionate individuals. If parents do not lay down the rules and interpret them consistently, it takes longer for their children to learn how to behave. By testing rules and boundaries children are trying to learn about the world about them.

SOCIAL INTERACTION
Children learn to enjoy helping adults in daily tasks such as cooking, shopping and gardening, and get pleasure and fulfilment from co-operating and achieving things with adults.

Children also set up their own social networks. They want to be with other children and have friends. First of all children play with anyone who is doing what they are doing but later they start making real friends.

UNDERSTANDING THE FEELINGS OF OTHERS
Children sense the feelings of others, whether they are upset, sad, happy or angry. As they get older they are able to show that they understand the feelings of their friends by showing sympathy or concern, say if they hurt themselves or if they are made unhappy by an event. Children need to temper their own natural egocentricity with an interest in others and an empathy with their situation and concerns. If a child retains his egocentric view of the world into adulthood he will find it very difficult to make friends or interact socially because other people will not tolerate it for long.

PLAYING ALONE
Though social interaction is important, children need to balance it with time spent alone because this is important for relaxation and for experimentation. As adults, we spend time alone to experiment and rehearse what we are going to say or how we are going to behave before we feel confident to do so publicly. Children spend short periods playing alone initially but will gradually extend their solitary play and want to go off to their own space to play for longer periods.

LEARNING SOCIAL RULES

Children learn to copy adults and to want to co-operate with them and win their approval. As their social circle extends and they make their own friends, and as they discover what is permissible behaviour and what is not, they learn to obey the social rules more generally and fit in with other people.

Parallel development

PERSONALITIES

Children are born with their own personalities – some are shy and intro-verted and others are extrovert and gregarious. Children's personalities should always be respected and allowed to develop with under-standing.

SOCIAL PLAY

To begin with, children play on their own but, over time, they learn to play with others in a co-operative way. This process is very gradual, so though usually differentiated in the following way it may not be easy to 'classify' a child at any one time. Genuine co-operative play is the goal, but we probably all know some 'normal' adults who aren't very good at it!

Solitary play

A child plays on his own, for example posting shapes, pushing cars or doing puzzles.

Parallel play

A child plays alongside another child but with no interaction between them. For instance, two children play in a sand pit digging and pouring sand. Both are doing the same thing but not together.

Observing play

A child becomes aware of what others are doing and is interested in it but does not actually join in. If a child goes into a playgroup and sees some children playing with Duplo, he will stop and watch them from the edge but not take the plunge and join in. Although this is identified as a separate phase, children do observe others at earlier phases of their development too.

Joining in

Children play together doing the same activity but on their own terms, so although they may dress up together or help each other play with Duplo they will often end up being aggressive towards each other.

Co-operative play

This is genuinely co-operative play where children have negotiated a way of sharing an activity with each other and are able to resolve most disagreements and differences themselves. They are prepared to wait, take turns and share. For instance, they may play hide and seek with each other or Snap cards. This is highly developed play.

IMAGINATIVE PLAY

Imaginative play is one of the ways in which children explore social situations. They may act out situations they have witnessed or take on different roles. It is also an important vehicle for them to interact with their peers by co-operating with them to act out different scenarios. It is covered more fully in Chapter 3, pp.60–61.

Games and activities

Chronological development

INTEREST IN PEOPLE

Some children with special needs are withdrawn and uninterested in people, but they need to learn that there is a point to human contact.

- Play eye contact games to encourage your child to interact with adults. Many different games are listed in Chapter 4, pp.90–93. Make sure you give your child time to respond.

- Play any game which your child likes, because if he enjoys it he will see the point of interacting with you. In addition, if he wants to play the game again, he will have to find a way of communicating that desire. When you play, try to incorporate lots of eye contact and physical contact.

- While looking in the mirror with your child, make exaggerated and interesting faces, silly expressions and funny noises, and play peek-a-boo games. Any games with mirrors will make a child look at his own and other faces.

Make eye contact

- Dress up in silly clothes, such as hats, earrings, glasses and false noses to gain attention.
- Play with sound-making toys near your face to draw attention to yourself.
- Use face paints to make your face more interesting.
- Also use the ideas listed in the section on getting a response in Chapter 8, pp.193–194.

ANTICIPATION OF FAMILIAR ACTIVITIES

In daily life try to establish good routines to give your child a better chance of understanding what is happening and anticipating what is about to happen. Try to give clues as to what is going to happen – for example, the sound of running taps for a bath, a plate and spoon before meal-times, a certain location for nappy changes and so on.

Try to keep certain toys in a particular room so that your child can learn where things are kept.

Use the same language to describe things each day. Don't vary it too much because it makes it more difficult to understand.

CONCEPT OF SELF-IDENTITY
Play games which give your child an awareness of his body and himself. Ideas for games are described in Chapter 8, pp.196–197.

TURN-TAKING
Ideas for games to aid anticipation and turn-taking are listed in Chapter 4, p.94.

GETTING ADULT ATTENTION
Before being able to talk, your child can request your attention in a number of ways, for example by eye pointing, finger or hand pointing, offering a toy, tugging at you or your clothes, using natural gesture, taking your hand to an object, leading you to something or vocalizing. All methods are really helpful to you and him and show his desire for communication and social interaction.

Taking an adult by the hand

Respond to him immediately, acknowledge his request and give an immediate response whether it is a yes or a no. If he doesn't get a response from you, he might stop asking and become more withdrawn. If your child tries to interact in any way:

- respond immediately and if possible give him what he wants since it will encourage him to try again

- be exaggerated in your response so he gets a big reward, either by being excessive yourself, with lots of noise and facial expressions or, if you have a large family or a group of friends round, get them to join in the response.

It can be difficult to be sure that your child is actually trying to communicate by eye pointing or a slight gesture but it is better to give him the benefit of the doubt. Even if he isn't it might encourage him to try and won't do any harm. If you take a negative view you may be ignoring his efforts.

Early communication skills are described more fully in Chapter 4, pp.83–87.

CO-OPERATING IN GAMES WITH AN ADULT

- Get your child to give you objects and toys. Hold out your hand and ask for whatever he has in his hands at the time and see if he will release it into your hands.
- Roll a ball or car between you and your child.
- Play 'Round and round the garden' and get him to hold out his hand in readiness for you (see p.95 for words).
- Try any singing games where your child has to co-operate with you with his movements. You might:
  ○ Hold your child's hands in yours and get him to clap singing 'pat-a-cake' (see p.63) or other clapping songs.
  ○ Sing 'My hands and your hands' over and over again while alternately clapping your own hands together and then clapping your child's.

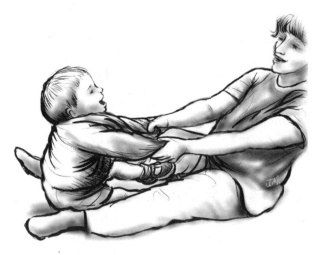

Row, row, row your boat

- ○ Sing 'Row, row, row your boat' or 'See-saw Margery Daw' (the words are on p.92). Hold your child's hands and pretend to row so that he has to co-operate with your movements.

- ○ Similarly, you can use 'Have you ever ever ever in your long legged life' (see p.92 for words). Lay your child on his back and, holding his ankles, move his legs round and round with bent knees in a cycling motion.

- ○ Hold your child on your knee, facing you, and with the palms of your hands together sway to:

  > My bonny lies over the ocean
  > My bonny lies over the sea
  > My bonny lies over the ocean
  > Oh bring back my bonny to me
  > Bring back, bring back
  > Oh bring back my bonny to me, to me
  > Bring back, bring back
  > Oh bring back my bonny to me.

- ○ Use any rhyme with a beat to sway or row together. Or hold your child in your arms and hum, swaying to the music.

- Play tug of war games. For example, use a rope with hoops on it which he can see moving from one end to the other as each of you pulls the rope in turn.

- Use opportunities as they arise for 'to and fro' games. For instance, if your child pulls you back by a rucksack strap or a shirt tail, move forwards and wait for him to pull you back. These situations just arise naturally and can be useful opportunities for interaction.

COPYING AN ADULT

In social situations, show your child what to do and what is expected of him. But don't expect him to co-operate for long. If you want him to sit down to drink his milk, sit down yourself and drink your coffee. Set a good example in all things!

Other ideas for copying are included in Chapter 3, pp.62–64 and Chapter 4, p.97.

SHARING AND TURN-TAKING

As children start interacting with others, they have to develop an ability to share and take turns. You have to insist that your child obeys the rules and does not snatch toys away from others but allows others to use his toys and belongings. You also have to ensure that others do the same for him so that he can see the benefits of obeying the rules. Make sure, therefore, that you are fair and even-handed and that other adults do the same for your child.

- Have a teddy bears' picnic and get your child to share food fairly between the participants.

- If you go out to feed the ducks make a conscious effort to give some to one duck and then some to another and some more to another and so on.

- Share out food at meal-times – some for John, some for Jane, some for Mummy and some for Daddy. Share out things like raisins or sweets like Smarties and chocolate buttons.

- Get your child to play turn-taking games with his peers such as siblings or friends at home or in playgroups. This will give him an opportunity to learn to obey simple social rules. Playgroups and playgrounds can be very good for this because children have to wait their turns to use equipment like trampolines, slides or swings and to learn to give things up for others. Again, make sure your child is getting a fair deal.

TESTING THE BOUNDARIES

Techniques for behaviour management are covered in detail in Chapter 9, pp.202–211.

SOCIAL INTERACTION

Get your child to help you in everyday activities like tucking in sheets, using a dustpan and brush, polishing furniture, cooking, pushing a pushchair jointly, or carrying a basket or bag jointly.

UNDERSTANDING THE FEELINGS OF OTHERS

Take every opportunity to talk about emotions as they come up in daily life or in books and videos.

For other ideas for activities see Chapter 8, pp.200–201.

PLAYING ALONE

Select a toy or game that your child enjoys and can play without adult help. Sit in the same room and talk him through the game but do not get physically involved. Aim for only a few minutes to begin with. Gradually say less and extend the time period.

Playing alone

Find an interesting book or photograph album and encourage your child to look at it by himself but stay nearby.

LEARNING SOCIAL RULES

Children take time to learn what is acceptable behaviour in different circumstances and situations.

Avoid social situations which your child cannot handle if this is at all possible. There is no point putting you and him through stressful situations if they are not necessary. For example, you don't have to take your child to a posh restaurant when a pizza place would do. When your child's behaviour has improved you can try again.

There are some situations which are unavoidable, like hospital visits and shoe shopping. When you are faced with these, try the following ideas:

- Talk your child through every situation very simply, involve him in what is going on and give him something to concentrate on. If you are going round the supermarket, talk about what you are buying, what colour it is, its size and qualities and anticipate what you are going to buy next. People may think you are slightly odd but that is better than having an hysterical child.

- Give your child something to do in a situation which is likely to throw him. If your child always misbehaves in certain shops give him a special toy as you go in, as this may distract him for a while.

- If you are going shopping, give your child his own shopping list made with pictures or labels so he can get some things by himself.

- If, for example, you are going on a holiday or your child is going into hospital prepare him for the new experience by talking about what is going to happen and by showing him relevant pictures, photographs or books.

- If you are having problems with specific situations start off by practising at home, then introduce other people into the exercise before taking your child out to a friend's house and finally into a normal situation. For example, you might be having problems getting your child to sit still to eat meals in strange environments because he finds it too interesting or disturbing. So going to birthday parties or out for meals is very difficult. Start by being firm at home about sitting down to eat or drink. When friends come round insist on the same behaviour. When you go to a friend's house do the same and when you have the behaviour established, attempt a bigger gathering – a birthday party, playgroup tea or restaurant meal. Build up the time spent sitting at the table.

- You could try making up a Social Story™ to change a particular behaviour (Gray and Leigh White 2002). Social Stories™ are simple illustrated narratives describing a particular situation from your child's point of view and giving him a set of actions to follow. The Story is personalized by using the appropriate names, situation and illustrations. It should provide a context, state the right behaviour, the behaviour you wish to stop and end on a positive note. The following is an example of a Social Story™.

> ### Christopher's Story – Kissing
>
> We kiss people to show them that we love them.
>
> Christopher kisses his Mummy, Daddy, Nick and Billy.
>
> Christopher might kiss other people in his family.
>
> Christopher can kiss Floppy Duck because he is soft and cuddly and he loves it.
>
> We don't kiss paper or pencils or other things in school.
>
> I will try not to kiss paper and other things. I am a good boy.

You could use Social Stories™ to address a variety of issues for example going to the toilet, throwing things or how to behave in the car. You can then read the story to your child at different times so that he can learn how to behave in this particular situation. Social Stories™ covering a wide range of issues and situations appropriate to very young children are described in 'My Social Stories Book' (see references, p.266). Social Stories™ can be very successful, particularly with more able children.

Ultimately it may be repeated experience of a situation which makes a child understand what he is or is not supposed to do. In the end there may be nothing you can do but persevere using behaviour management techniques to reinforce good behaviour. See Chapter 9, p.204.

When my son first had to wear glasses he used to go berserk in the opticians – trying on all the glasses, pulling the contact lens solutions off the shelf, trying to play with the till etc. despite the fact that it had a lovely play area for children. After six months of constant visits (because he was forever breaking his glasses), he has learnt to behave better and will head for the play area straightaway.

Parallel development

GENDER ISSUES

Don't stereotype your child. Give him the opportunity to play with toys of all kinds and to do all sorts of activities regardless of gender. Allow and encourage boys to play with dolls and to cook and allow and encourage girls to play with train sets and cars.

DEVELOPING SOCIAL PLAY

Before you start on social play, make sure the fundamentals of eye contact, turn-taking and co-operation are well established.

Parallel play (playing alongside another child)
Children first play with an adult because adults are more predictable and controllable than other children, so the first step towards getting your child to play alongside another is to get him to play alongside you. Copy what he does, so if he crawls, you crawl; if he builds a tower with bricks you do the same.

Respect a child's sense of personal space. The amount of personal space we need is affected by cultural factors and some children with special needs, such as autistic children, also need greater space than others.

Get your child to participate in a singing session at a playgroup or mother and toddler group – these will require him to play alongside another child in a non-threatening way.

Go to playgrounds and encourage your child to play on the slides, swings and climbing frames because they are a good starting point for a child to play alongside other children.

Encourage your child to do some constructive play that he enjoys while another child is doing the same thing; for example, Duplo, painting, drawing, sand and water play. Contrary to what might be expected, children co-operate better in a controlled environment than during free time. If your child has siblings of a suitable age then they would be the obvious first playmates because they are familiar and you will find plenty of opportunities to share games. Alternatively, you could set up play with children whom he sees regularly at home or at playgroup.

Joining in play (playing with another child)
Once your child is playing alongside other children happily, interaction may come over time.

Try simple and easy games such as peek-a-boo games or turn-taking games (putting marbles in a marble run, running cars down a shoot). It's also good to try a game where there are two interdependent actions. One child might do one element and the other child completes it. For example, one child puts an object in and the other presses a switch for it to fall out.

When your child with special needs joins in with his peers, you may have to consider how he is treated. Children with special needs are often in danger of either being 'mothered' by other children or being bullied and teased. It is up to the playgroup and parents to set the tone and to give children the understanding to treat children with special needs with compassion but also with respect. Don't be afraid to point things out to others; they're probably oblivious to the problem.

CHAPTER 8

Emotional Development

The theory

What is emotional development?

Emotional development in the early years involves a child gaining an awareness of herself. She learns that she is a separate individual, that she has a body and a name and that she can influence and affect her environment and the people around her. Her personality and her early upbringing jointly lay the foundations for how she will feel about herself later in life, her self-esteem, confidence and behaviour. Later she will learn that she and other people have different emotions at different times and how to deal with them.

Chronological development

THE NEWBORN BABY

Newborn babies seek human contact and comfort. Initially they can only cry to show that they want attention and company. But they soon learn to smile and vocalize and, if parents respond quickly and appropriately, discover that this behaviour is more useful for getting attention and entertainment (Holmes 1993).

LOVE

All children need love and security. They need adults who are responsive to them. Children need to be in a loving and secure environment where they feel safe and valued and therefore have the confidence to take risks, make mistakes and learn from them.

Unconditional love

Children who are not secure may become withdrawn or timid or, more likely, become badly behaved or even aggressive in an effort to gain adult attention. These children will need more love and should be given attention for the positive things that they do rather than for their trans- gressions (see Chapter 9, p.204). Children need enough stimulation, then time to think and respond; they do not need over-stimulation.

Children, however, should not be overprotected and smothered in love. They need to have the space to gain independence from their family.

RESPONDING TO PHYSICAL CONTACT
After they have learnt to smile, children start to enjoy more active physical contact like cuddles, tickles and gentle physical play. They show their enjoyment by smiling, vocalizing and later chuckling and laughing.

PHYSICAL SELF-AWARENESS
A baby initially has no real concept of herself as a physical and separate person. She may just see herself as an extension of her mother's body. She will gradually learn that she has her own body and where it begins and ends.

Children start to explore what their hands can do by passing them in front of their face, playing with their fingers and working out that they can control them. Similarly, they bring their feet up and investigate them by putting them in their mouth. As children develop physically and are able to sit up, crawl and walk, they learn more about themselves and their bodies.

These experiments give children an understanding of what and where their bodies are and how they can control them. They underlie emotional development since a child needs an understanding of her physical body before she can have any notion of her mind and emotions.

CONCEPT OF SELF

Children gain an awareness of themselves as individuals with their own minds. They play peek-a-boo games and become aware that things continue to exist even when they cannot be seen. They start to recognize and respond to their own names.

DEPENDENCE ON A FAMILIAR ADULT

Children initially like adult company but are not heavily dependent on their mother or principal carer. They can be passed from one adult to another and later play contentedly by themselves. As they become more aware of things going on around them, they become more anxious and will tend to cling to their mother if she tries to leave them. As children gain greater confidence and a sense of security they will once again tolerate being left.

SHARING ·

As children gain an understanding of who they are, they also become aware of what belongs to them, and can be quite possessive about their toys, their parents and their environment. It takes time before they develop an ability to share things with other children and to take turns.

RECOGNIZING THEMSELVES

When children first see themselves in a mirror, they think their reflection is another person and try to touch it and interact with it. However eventually they recognize themselves in the mirror and in photographs.

They also soon start acquiring an idea of their body image – whether they are a boy or a girl, whether they are tall or short, and so on. They detect differences between other people and themselves very early on so it is important that their self-esteem is built up from an early age.

SELF-ESTEEM

Children need to develop their self-esteem in order to gain the confidence to leave the family environment and take risks in their social, educational and work life. Children who have high self-esteem tend to feel more fulfilled and happier as adults than those who do not.

Parents are the first and most important people to contribute towards generating self-esteem. By praising their child for what she has done rather than telling her off for what she has not, by valuing her achievements – whether they are attempts to talk or pictures exhibited on the fridge – and by giving her the trust, freedom, space and opportunity to venture out and try new experiences, parents contribute to their child's perception of her abilities and their value.

Choices are also important in a child's life. A child who is never given any choice in what she does may become passive or confrontational. Being able to make choices is an important skill in itself; but it is also one of the things that makes our lives worth living. It gives us our sense of control, independence and autonomy.

Children therefore need to make choices in their lives. At a simple level it may be the choice between an apple and banana for pudding or different books or toys to play with. Later, when they have the understanding, children can be asked to make more complex choices such as whether they want to go swimming or to the park.

Children also need to learn to be able to cope with not succeeding and to develop ways of accepting their failures, putting them in perspective, learning from them and trying again. Children pick up their parents' attitudes to failure by seeing how they respond. If a child is having difficulty getting dressed, she could either throw her clothes down in frustration or try again perhaps seeking parental help. She may make this decision based on seeing how her own parents react to things going wrong.

SENSE OF SECURITY

Parents set boundaries for what is acceptable behaviour for their children. Children test those boundaries and ideally find that they are consistent and immovable. Children then know what is expected of them. They also feel that their parents are in control not only of their own family but also of the wider world too. This gives children a sense of security and safety which helps their emotional development. This does not mean, however, that children cannot have choices within those boundaries.

If the boundaries are always shifting, children don't know what is expected of them and they will feel insecure. In addition, children will see that their parents can be controlled by them, in which case their parents can't possibly be in control of their own family circle – let alone the world beyond.

FEARS
At some point most children are afraid of falling or of strangers. Later they can develop other fears. Some are rational like a fear of dogs if they have been bitten; some are acquired from other people, like a fear of spiders acquired from a parent; and others are irrational, like a fear of monsters or of falling down the toilet. These last fears often come as their imagination develops ahead of their understanding of language and the world about them or from simple misunderstandings. For example, a small child became frightened of going to bed at night. It transpired that she was frightened by 'draughts'. She had no understanding of what a draught was, but her mother said each night 'I'll tuck you up nice and tight to keep the draughts out' and so she was terrified!

UNDERSTANDING AND EXPRESSING EMOTIONS
Children grow to recognize emotions in other people like anger, happiness, pain and surprise. They later learn to respond appropriately by seeking to comfort others who have hurt themselves or expressing happiness at another child's birthday. Children learn to express emotions such as affection for brothers and sisters. They also learn which emotions it is not socially acceptable to express. For example, for many people in our culture boys aren't supposed to cry and girls shouldn't express open aggression. It is debatable whether this is a good thing or not.

Whether children grow up to be assertive and able to say 'no' to other people, to be passive and heavily influenced by others or to be aggressive and bully others is influenced by their parents and by their innate personality.

GROWING INDEPENDENCE
Children gradually gain independence from their parents. They get to a stage when they want to do everything by themselves but they can't because it's not safe or they don't have the physical capability. This often leads to temper tantrums because they don't understand why

their activities are being curtailed. However, as they develop their skills and their understanding, they may safely do more by themselves.

Space to gain independence

Games and activities

Chronological development

GETTING A RESPONSE

Some children with special needs are unresponsive and uninterested in people and their environment. This is one of the hardest things for parents to cope with. Parents usually strive both subconsciously and consciously to find things that will elicit a response from their child and it is vitally important that parents of unresponsive and passive children do not reject their child but continue to show them affection by smiling, talking and cuddling them and by seeking activities which they may enjoy.

> Before we even knew our son had problems we had found instinc-tively that the one thing that seemed to elicit a response was tickling games and we used to play them a lot. The first time he ever initiated play with us was when, at about 18 months, he held out his hand by himself as a request for more 'Round and round the garden'. It was a wonderful moment.

Often you may find yourself wondering if what gives pleasure to your child is of any use to her, whether it is tickling, bubbles or rough play. It is. To see your child enjoying herself is not only wonderful in itself for you but it is also a spur and a stimulation to all sorts of other activities for

Don't reject an unresponsive child

her. A child who likes bubbles may learn to point to or say 'bubbles', or to crawl to the bubbles, or to play at bubbles with other children.

You will know when your child is responding to something that is going on, even if the response is very slight. Build on it.

Below are some ideas for activities which might appeal to your child. Remember that children with special needs often take longer to respond so give your child plenty of time.

GET YOUR CHILD'S ATTENTION
First of all get your child's attention by doing something out of the ordinary which will alert her to the fact that something unusual is about to happen. A visual prompt like putting on an extravagant hat is probably the easiest. You could also use some of the ideas for gaining eye contact listed in Chapter 4, pp.90–93.

Visually exciting toys
There are all sorts of things which might interest your child, for example very brightly coloured toys – and particularly those with flashing lights – also lights like torches, disco lights or fibre-optic lights. Children often love wind-up mechanical toys, friction cars and bubbles.

Physical play

- Play tickling games including 'Round and round the garden' and 'This little piggy'. For the words see Chapter 4, p.95.

- Do knee rides like 'Horsey, horsey don't you stop' and 'Humpty Dumpty'. For words and more examples see Chapter 4, pp.92 and 95.

- Cuddle her.

- Do some rough play, for example rolling your child around the bed, throwing her in the air and catching her, swirling her round and round in your arms and bouncing up and down holding her.

Sound

Use musical activities:

- Play any musical instrument whether it is the guitar, recorder, kazoo or drum.

- Sing nursery rhymes or your favourite pop song to your child.

- Play with musical toys like keyboards or musical spinning tops.

- Take your child to listen to live music – perhaps buskers in the street.

One day we were looking round Winchester Cathedral and happened to coincide with a rehearsal by the Bournemouth Symphony Orchestra. Our son was stunned by the sound of the full orchestra with the beautiful acoustics and we couldn't get him away.

Smell

- Try making 'smelly boxes'. Put aromatic substances like spices, coffee grains, tea or orange in a small box like a Tic-Tac box for your child to smell.

- Dab some perfume, aftershave, Dettol etc. on a ball of cotton wool and let your child smell it.

- Use aromatherapy oils.

Touch

- Find different textures on household objects to give your child different sensations – smooth (silk and velvet), rough, spiky (brush), lumpy, cold, warm, hard (stone), soft (fur), etc.

PHYSICAL SELF-AWARENESS

- Stroke, touch and massage parts of your child's body.
- Play with her hands and feet by holding and shaking them.
- Play gentle tickling games, for example, running your finger up the length of her body.
- Place your child in a confined space or near to a wall so that when she moves she makes contact with another surface.
- Give your child rattles, because when she moves her hand, she will have the movement reinforced by the sound. As well as hand-held rattles, you can use wrist rattles or mittens with bells sewn into them. Even if your child cannot grasp things she can still learn about her body. Similarly you can attach bells or small rattles to socks to encourage kicking.

CONCEPT OF SELF

The first body parts that a child learns to recognize are usually eyes, nose and mouth followed by hair, tummy and hands.

- Use opportunities as they come up naturally to name different body parts. Bath-time is the most obvious time as you wash each part, but you can also use nappy changing to name tummy, bottom, legs etc. and getting dressed to talk about arms, hands, feet etc.
- Sing songs such as 'Pat-a-cake', see p.63 for the words, or:

  Head and shoulders, knees and toes, knees and toes
  Head and shoulders, knees and toes, knees and toes
  And eyes and ears and mouth and nose
  Head, shoulders, knees and toes, knees and toes.

  Tommy thumb, Tommy thumb, where are you?
  Here I am, here I am and how do you do?
      Other verses:
      Peter pointer, Peter pointer, where are you?...
      Middle man, middle man, where are you?...
      Ruby ring, ruby ring, where are you?...
      Baby small, baby small, where are you?...

- Draw or use big clear pictures of faces and name the body parts.
- Sit your child on your knee and touch different parts of her body and your own as you name them, for example 'My knee. Your knee.'
- Use dolls to name body parts.
- Use mirrors to make your child look at herself while playing the following games:
    - Get her to touch different parts of her face.
    - Repeat her name as you point to her reflection.
    - Try putting a smudge of lipstick or shaving foam on her nose or cheeks. Either wipe it off yourself or get her to do it, so that she can appreciate that she is looking at herself.
    - Using a big mirror, make lots of silly faces and noises and see if you can encourage her to copy.
    - Play peek-a-boo games with the mirror, hiding the mirror then showing your child her face.

AWARENESS OF NAME

This requires a lot of repetition and perseverance. Name your child at every opportunity. Ask 'Where's Sophie? There's Sophie' while touching her chest with your finger and giving a big smile. Ask questions like: 'Who has got the ball? Jonathan's got the ball'.

Parents naturally talk to their child in the third person 'It's Jade's cup' rather than 'It's your cup'. This is good because it reinforces identity.

SHARING

- Play games where your child has to divide things between people and toys, for instance, a tea party for dolls or teddies where the food has to be given to each doll or teddy.
- Get your child to hand out food to other people as well as herself, for instance a biscuit for you and for her.

- Get your child to share some food or a toy with you or one other familiar person and get other children to do the same with her.

RECOGNIZING SELF IN MIRROR AND PHOTOGRAPHS
Use the mirror games described in the section on awareness of self (above) to encourage your child to see her own image and recognize it by pointing at it.

Use a mirror

Create a photograph album or a box of pictures of your family which your child can look at. It is good to use spare not-so-great photographs for this which you don't mind being damaged. Look through the album with your child naming the family members in each picture. Ask your child to find pictures of different people and of herself.

BUILDING UP SELF-ESTEEM
When a child has special needs and is aware of the difference between herself and other children, particularly perhaps because she has a physical disability or a sensory impairment, she needs even more support and encouragement to give her confidence and self-esteem.

Praise your child for her achievements. Children need masses of praise for things that they do and things that they try to do. Even if they do not always succeed, parents need to show appreciation for the effort shown. Children thrive on praise. They love the attention and will strive to repeat what they have done. It is a powerful motivator.

Show your appreciation of any work that your child has done. The fridge is a good place for a rotating exhibition but it is also good to have a noticeboard on which you can pin pictures and to display models and paintings round the room. Ask your child 'Who painted the picture? Yes, Jasmine did. It's beautiful.' Show them to family and friends and get them to join in the praise.

Use songs to increase self-esteem and confidence. Children generally find them enjoyable and fun and it's a non-threatening way of getting a child to do something which she cannot fail at. Songs with actions are particularly good because a child can join in with as little or as much as she is able and it does not matter if she cannot do it all. There are many examples in Chapter 3, pp.63–64, and Chapter 4, p.95. If you sing 'Wind the bobbin up', for example, and your child does the clapping you can praise that. Your child feels she has achieved something and everyone has enjoyed themselves. As the child's confidence and abilities grow, she will be able to do more.

Sing nursery rhymes and substitute your child's name in the song. For example sing 'Baa, baa black sheep' and instead of 'little boy who lives down the lane' sing 'little Ben who lives down the lane' or 'little Anna who lives down the lane'. Also try 'Rock-a-bye baby', singing 'Rock-a-bye Lauren on a tree top' or 'Rock-a-bye Nick Nick on a tree top'.

Encourage your child to play with water and sand because there is no right or wrong way to play – it is about exploring and experimenting.

Give your child good examples of how to cope with failure by your response to her failure and to your own. Show her that it is all right to fail and not to be very good at something and that it is the effort and the drive to try again that is valued.

Be positive in your approach as described in Chapter 2, pp.42–45.

Remember not to make praise valueless by overdoing it. If a skill is fairly well established you do not need to go overboard. Equally, if your child has not really made much of an effort then don't collude with her by praising her work. You will have to be sensitive to your child. If it is an achievement for your child to sit still and do any painting at all, praise her. If, on the other hand, your child is capable of sustained effort, don't praise a few marks on a piece of paper excessively.

MAKING A CHOICE
It is important to find ways of offering choices to children with special
needs and of enabling them to communicate their choice.

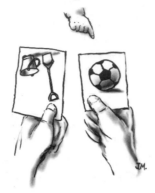

Use pictures to give your child a choice of activities

If you give your child a choice, she must be able to understand what you
are asking and be able to show in some way what she wants by eye
pointing, pointing, signing or speaking. To begin with, you may actually
need to have the objects in front of you so that she can clearly understand and select. To offer her a choice of fruit for tea, show her an apple
and a banana and ask which she would like. If she chooses an apple, by
eye pointing or pointing, hide the banana and say 'You want the apple'
and give it to her.

Easy choices are of food, drinks and games where you can show the
choice. For more complex choices you may have to show some wellies to
indicate going out or photographs or pictures of activities such as
swimming or going to the park.

UNDERSTANDING FEELINGS

- Show pictures of people expressing emotions and talk about
  them in simple language.

- Read books which show people expressing emotions.

- Explain what is happening around your child. 'He's hurt his
  knee. He's unhappy'. 'It's her birthday. She's happy'.

- If your child does something which affects someone else emotionally, explain it: 'You knocked him over. He's crying. Poor Oscar'.

- Use a mirror to show a happy face, a sad face, a surprised face, an angry face etc.

- Express emotions yourself and talk about them.

- Play imaginatively with your child, using different scenarios to show emotions such as dolly unwell or dolly falling over.

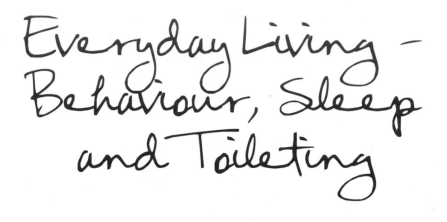

CHAPTER 9

Everyday Living – Behaviour, Sleep and Toileting

This chapter gives some brief advice on three aspects of life with children which are extremely important and can present challenges to children with special needs, namely behaviour, sleep and toileting.

Behaviour

There are many things that we can do as parents to encourage and enable good behaviour in our children. All children behave badly at times because they are tired, cross, thwarted or because they want to challenge the boundaries. Children with special needs can also demonstrate lots of poor or challenging behaviour. Coping with this can be difficult. You may find it tricky to establish the right balance between making allowances for a child's lack of understanding on the one hand, and being over strict in order to get her to conform and fit in on the other.

Strategies to enable good behaviour
SET STANDARDS OF GOOD BEHAVIOUR
Parents need to set limits of what is acceptable and unacceptable behaviour. The rules should be fair, predictable, consistent and understandable. Children will set out to find those limits and to test them to

see if they can be moved. Once they have found out the rules and have seen that they are enforced consistently they will know what is expected and what the consequences are of non-compliance. They will feel the world is predictable, ordered and controlled and this will enable them to feel secure and safe. Reasonable standards of behaviour enable children to become accepted in wider social circles which is vital for their development.

However, parents also need to make sure that there is enough freedom for children to explore and investigate so that they are not kept in a straightjacket but can experiment without fear of failure, learn and gain independence.

BE CONSISTENT

A child needs to know what the boundaries of acceptable behaviour are and she cannot if they are constantly changing. Some people sit down and decide what their house rules are and others will decide as they go along. If you decide that it is okay to stand on the sofa one day then you should not change your mind the next. Try to have a set of rules or guidelines and stick to them. If you are consistent, your child will find it much easier to understand what is expected and will learn more quickly how to behave appropriately.

HELP YOUR CHILD TO UNDERSTAND

Remember that young children have limited understanding and need as much help as possible to make sense of what is going on and what they are expected to do. Use a multi-sensory approach.

- Be a good role model. Try to model the behaviour you would like your child to emulate and ensure your other children do the same. It is no good telling your child to do one thing while you do the opposite.

- Use the suggestions in Chapter 2, Routines and predictability, pp.49–51, to give your child as much understanding as possible about her day. These give her a sense of security and clues as to how to behave.

- Make sure you are using language your child understands, for example use the same words each time and keep them simple (see p. for other suggestions). Reinforce it with a visual prompt such as a sign or symbol.

REWARD GOOD BEHAVIOUR

The golden rule of dealing with children's behaviour is to reward good behaviour and as far as possible to ignore bad behaviour. All the attention and praise should go to the behaviour you want to encourage. It does not help if you make a big issue of bad behaviour – your child may just enjoy all the attention and be encouraged to continue. We often praise children when they do something new and wonderful, and may get angry when they do something naughty. However, we tend not to acknowledge them when they are just doing what they are supposed to do, although this is, in fact, good behaviour which should be recognized. Try to praise and reward your child for just playing nicely or sitting still. Use the suggestions in Chapter 2, pp.42–44, on how to praise and encourage.

GIVE CHOICES

Children need some choice in their lives but the choices need to be appropriate to their level of understanding. There is little point asking a child whether she wants to go to France or Spain for her holiday since she will have no understanding of what this means. However, she might be able to understand the choice between wearing her yellow or red T-shirt.

It is also counter-productive to offer a child a choice when you know that only one option is viable or when you will overrule her choice. An example might be if you ask a child if she wants to go to the swings or to the beach; she decides on the beach and you then decide you want to go to the swings anyway. If there is not a genuine choice, do not give her the choice, just tell her what is going to happen.

However, choices within a child's abilities (what she wants to eat, which toys she wants to play with) are important for a child's self-esteem, independence and life skills. It is also important that parents recognize that children have views and desires and that these should be respected. A child who is deprived of choice in her life may become passive or badly behaved.

How to change persistent bad behaviour

If poor behaviour is a regular problem you could address it in the following way using behaviour management techniques.

LOOK AT WHAT THE BEHAVIOUR MEANS

Behaviour always has a function and bad behaviour is often a form of communication in any child. For a child with communication problems it may be one of the few ways available for her to get her message across and it is probably the most effective. If your child is behaving badly look at what she is 'saying' to you or what the function of the behaviour is.

You could use the ABCC of behaviour:

- A= Antecedents. What led up to the bad behaviour?
- B= Behaviour. What did she do and how did you respond?
- C= Consequences. What were the consequences for the child?
- C= Communication Intent. What was she trying to tell you?

Example

A child might be playing nicely and then starts attacking her baby sister, so you tell her off and distract her with a new activity.

- Antecedents = She has been playing on her own for some time. Your attention is largely going to her little sister.
- Behaviour = She behaves badly by yanking her sister's hair, you get very angry and shout at her.
- Consequences = She gets lots of attention and a change of activity.
- Communication Intent = She was bored and wanted some attention and to do something different.

In other situations bad behaviour might mean 'I don't know how to handle this situation', 'I want to be left alone', 'This is too difficult', 'I can't bear this loud noise', 'I love spinning around' or 'I am tired'.

Once you have unravelled the background to the behaviour and what the behaviour was communicating, you might be able to see a solution. It may be that your child is getting hungry and you need to make sure you have a snack with you. It may be that she cannot bear the sound of the Hoover and you need to do the hoovering when she is not around or you may need to give her time to switch off.

LOOK FOR PATTERNS OF BAD BEHAVIOUR

If your child's poor behaviour seems overwhelming and non-stop, you could keep a behaviour diary to identify all the incidents during the day. When you examine it you may well see that there are particular situations, events or inputs which trigger the bad behaviour.

SOME COMMON ISSUES AFFECTING BEHAVIOUR

Sensory issues

Remember that your child may have a problem with sensory integration and her bad behaviour may be because she cannot bear the information that her senses are giving her, such as the texture of her clothes, loud noises or bright lights, or because she craves stimulation such as banging or jumping. These needs should be respected. See Chapter 6, pp.154–155, for further information.

Communication

Since bad behaviour is often used as a form of communication, it is really important to concentrate on helping your child to communicate through other means such as language, signs or pictures so that she can express herself and get her needs met without resorting to bad behaviour. If your child is very frustrated by her inability to communicate it may be worth considering introducing PECS (see Chapter 4, p.111, for further information).

IDENTIFY THE MOST IMPORTANT ISSUES TO TACKLE

For your own sanity, concentrate on no more than two or three major problems at any one time, for instance running off in the car park and pulling hair. It is impossible to tackle all behaviour issues at once, so choose those which are the most dangerous or difficult to live with.

When you have decided which issue to tackle, devise a plan of action incorporating the following ideas:

- Be consistent.
- Say no – be firm.
- Do not give in however much your child persists.
- Find an alternative activity which your child can do instead of continuing with the problem behaviour.
- Respond immediately.
- Reward her when she behaves well.

Be consistent

Decide which issue you are going to tackle and make sure that you are consistent in your approach. If you say your child must not play with your CDs, you must always intervene, not let it go sometimes because you are busy or cannot face it. Make sure everyone who cares for your child – grandparents, playgroups and childminders – follows the same approach, so that she has total consistency.

Say 'no' quietly but firmly

When your child does something unacceptable like hit another child or pinch biscuits, say 'no' quietly and firmly with a hand movement to reinforce it. Do not make a fuss, do not get angry and upset. She will then understand that her behaviour is unacceptable but she does not see you wound up and annoyed.

Never give in

If you have said no you must stick to your decision and not give in because children must learn that when you say 'no' you mean 'no'. If a child knows that you will give in if she persists, you are going to make matters worse for yourself.

Think of the child who keeps demanding biscuits. If you have a policy of giving just one, the child soon learns and will not persist once she has had her ration. If, on the other hand, you sometimes give in, she knows that if she whines on sufficiently she may eventually get her extra biscuit.

If your child throws a tantrum, ignore it. Don't remonstrate or reason with your child, just ignore her and wait for her to emerge from her tantrum. Never let it succeed, otherwise your child will learn that it is a good way to get what she wants and she will throw a tantrum every time she is thwarted.

If you start to use these ideas of behaviour management you may find things seem more difficult before they get better because your child will be determined to break down your resistance and find out where those boundaries are. Be strong, stay firm and persevere.

Find a distraction or alternative

Try to distract her by showing her a different toy or activity or by offering her an alternative activity. For example, if your child pulls hair, say 'no' and then suggest that she stroke the child's hair instead – it is difficult to stroke and pull at the same time. You could also suggest she stamp her feet rather than kick. It helps to find something positive she can do rather than just focusing on the negative.

Some situations which trigger bad behaviour are unavoidable so you have to develop a strategy for dealing with them. These are often when you cannot give attention or when a child does not understand what is happening. Find something to distract or occupy your child when the inevitable happens. For example, if your child is naughty when you are talking on the phone, have a box of special toys which you keep nearby to give her when the phone rings. See the section on learning social rules in Chapter 7, pp.183–185, for other ideas.

> We tried a special mat for Douglas and whenever he became so hyped-up that he was out of control we put him on it to calm down. He soon found it so helpful that he would ask to sit on it when he recognized that he was losing control. Later it became a magical mat which took him off to exotic lands.

Respond immediately
You should respond immediately to bad behaviour, otherwise your child will not understand what you are talking about.

If your child behaves badly at a party, pinching other children's food for instance, you must tell her off straightaway and if necessary remove her, not wait till you get home and say 'You were very naughty at the party', when she will have no idea what you mean. Even if you were to say 'You were very naughty pinching little Johnny's food at the party', she may still not be able to make the connection. You must make a very direct and immediate response.

You must also remember that when you praise your child or tell her off you must tell her what she is doing that is right or wrong. Rather than say 'good girl' or 'naughty girl' you should say 'good eating' or 'no, no hair pulling'. This way you are reinforcing your message. If you just say 'good' or 'bad' she does not necessarily know what she is being praised or criticized for. For the child's self-esteem it is important that you criticize the behaviour and not the child.

Reward her good behaviour
Reward your child when she stops and does what you want. You might think that in order to encourage good behaviour you should come down heavily on your child and 'discipline' bad behaviour. But it doesn't work. The key is to ignore bad behaviour. If you make a big fuss of bad behav-

iour, your child will get exactly what she wants, which is attention, and will have every incentive to carry on. If, on the other hand, you ignore bad behaviour, your child will achieve nothing. But at the same time you must give her attention when she behaves well. Find the rewards that motivate your child. It probably will not be what you would choose. For some, praise, cuddles and smiles or a star chart will be motivating, for others it might be bubbles, tickles, a ride in the car, the opportunity to rip paper or gain a football card to add to their collection. You know your child: find something she loves however strange it may seem.

Maya loves the Tweenies and so her reward for good behaviour was a piece of a Tweenie puzzle. She was gradually able to complete the pictures of the different Tweenies every time she was rewarded for being good.

Other issues
MODIFYING INAPPROPRIATE BEHAVIOUR
Children with special needs can often learn behaviours which need to be changed later. Sometimes they learn to do something which is fine at the time but which they then use indiscriminately in a manner which you think is inappropriate. An example is if a child learns to kiss but then kisses everyone from granny to the gas man.

Inappropriate behaviour: kissing the gas man

If your child has learnt a behaviour which you wish to change you will need to find an alternative action which you can show your child instead. So the child who kisses everybody could be shown how to say or sign 'hello' and the child who applauds could be shown how to say or sign 'good'.

Bouncing on furniture may be fine when your child is small but not so acceptable as she gets older. Try to change her behaviour gradually by saying she cannot bounce on the chairs, only on the sofa, then later only on her bed, progressing to only on the trampoline at playgroup.

SELF-HARM
Some children harm themselves, for example by head-banging, biting themselves or pulling their hair out. This can be dangerous and is very distressing for parents to witness.

If your child does harm herself, try to find the reason why. It might be frustration because of her inability to make herself understood, but could be because she is frightened or confused. Perhaps she is trying to make you understand something, but she can't; then she tries again, and still she can't, until she is so upset she either attacks someone else or herself. You must try to read her message before she gets so upset and angry. So use the methods described above. Look at when such behaviour is likely to happen and avoid those situations occurring.

If you cannot prevent the situation occurring have a distraction ready for your child straightaway. Failing that give her something else to vent her anger on like a pillow to punch or a squeaky toy to bite.

If you cannot prevent the self-harm occurring, intervene to stop your child from causing too much harm but try not to draw attention to it. As your child is better able to understand what is going on and communicate her needs, the self-harm will probably diminish.

> Hannah kept biting her wrists with frustration. We made armbands from old shoulder pads and Velcro and although she still bit into them it was easier to ignore as there was no blood! Eventually she stopped biting.

OBSESSIONS
If your child has interests which are obsessional, allow her to pursue the ones which are safe and acceptable to you, even if irritating, and only stop those which are dangerous and anti-social. You cannot stop a child having obsessions, so if you stop one she will only find another. Children with autism in particular will feel more secure if they know they will have time to indulge their obsessions. If they are denied they

become anxious and seek to indulge them all the time, because they never know when the next opportunity will arise. So timetable short periods of their favoured activity, whether water play, spinning or swinging, using a visual timetable.

Strategies for parents to cope with their child's poor behaviour

Parents can find that the behaviour of their child with special needs is very difficult to cope with because family, friends and other people generally are not aware of their child's problems and how they affect her behaviour. In addition everybody has different priorities and different standards. People find it easy to see where a child fails to come up to their own standards but rarely notice when her behaviour exceeds them. Don't worry about other people's views. Just work on your own priorities.

Don't make life any more difficult for yourself than necessary. If your child fiddles with your precious ornaments or CDs just put them out of reach or away. If there is an easy solution, use it.

Try to remain positive. For every negative thing you say make sure you find at least one positive thing to say to your child. Ensure that you begin and end each day on a positive note.

If your child has behavioural problems it can be very stressful. Try to find activities which your child enjoys and for which she behaves well, like going swimming or to the swings, and make sure you do them quite frequently so you have some positive times together.

Find activities which your child enjoys

Sleep

If you are happy with your child's sleeping (or non-sleeping) habits then carry on and ignore other people's comments. They are only a problem if you think they are a problem. If, however, you do decide that you are fed up with your child staying up late, having disturbed nights, waking early in the mornings or with finding your child in your bed with you then you are being perfectly reasonable to want to change things. It is within everyone's rights to expect a decent night's sleep. This is true for you and your child.

Parents need some time in the evening for their own activities as well as a good night's rest. It is much easier to cope if you know that at seven or eight o'clock your child will go to bed and stay there until a reasonable time in the morning. For your child, learning to go to sleep on her own and to sleep through the night is a vital life skill. We all feel much better after a good night's sleep.

If you are going to tackle sleep habits you must be ready and determined. The most important rule is that once you have started you must not stop because if you do you will send completely the wrong message to your child i.e. that she can control you, rather than that you control her, and next time you attempt to control her sleeping habits it will be even more difficult.

If you decide to change your child's sleeping habits you will probably find things get worse before they get better. You will probably get less sleep in the short term and at night, when you are tired, you will have to cope emotionally and physically with seeing your child unhappy and distressed. It is probably best to leave sleep training until you are so fed up that you are determined to sort it out once and for all. However, if there is any other reason why it might be particularly difficult to leave a child to cry – for example, someone is unwell or you have friends staying whom you don't want disturbed – it will weaken your resolve. Put sleep training off until you are ready.

- Make sure your partner and other members of the family are in support; follow your plan and if possible share the burden so that you can get some sleep.

- Be prepared for it to take some time, but be confident that all habits can be changed if you are strong enough and consistent enough.

The theory of sleep training

Children need to learn to go to sleep on their own. This is the most crucial element and from it stems all good practice. You should be able to leave your child in her cot or bed awake and let her go to sleep. Children will naturally wake during the night but they should be able to resettle themselves without having to wake you up for comfort, cuddles or company until they go back to sleep (Polke and Thompson 1994).

If your child has problems either going to sleep in the first place or waking in the night, you should consider whether or not she is actually able to go to sleep on her own. Look at her sleep routine and see if she has formed a habit of only falling asleep in certain circumstances, e.g. when you are present, if she has a bottle, if she is in your bed or if watching TV. If this is the case, then it shows that when she is waking in the night she is not able to get back to sleep because she has not got her particular prop. You will have to tackle the 'going to sleep' routine as well as waking in the night.

The practice of sleep training

BED-TIME ROUTINE

Establish a good routine before bed, for example a bath, a book and then bed. Don't make it overlong and don't play rough and tumble games which will excite and stimulate her. Make it soothing, relaxing and comforting.

When it is time to leave her, say goodnight and leave in a confident way. Mean business.

Ensure that the problem is not a practical one. Check that she is not too hot or too cold (continental-style sleeping-bag pyjamas or an extra layer of fleecy all-in-ones are good ways of keeping warm a child who always kicks off her blankets). Make sure she is not hungry at night by offering extra milk or something filling like a fromage frais at tea time. Some children with sensory integration disorder are very aware of how their bedclothes feel – the texture and the weight – so some might like to feel very weighed down with heavy blankets and others might prefer the opposite.

SETTLING DOWN

If your child will not settle on her own, there are two main strategies. Choose the one which best suits your situation and temperament.

1. Once you have settled your child leave her. If she gets up just keep taking her back to bed saying 'time for bed'. You will have to carry on doing this for as long as it takes. The first night it may be 20 times but the next night it may be only a few because once she has learned that she is not going to gain anything she will give up and go to sleep.

    If your child is in a cot and stands up and wails on being left, check and resettle her every five minutes or so (extending the time to ten and fifteen minutes) until she goes to sleep.

2. Alternatively, you can sit with your child until she falls asleep but each night position yourself further away from her. To begin with sit on the bed, then the next day on the floor by the bed, then further away until you are in the doorway, then on the landing, then just upstairs or nearby until she falls asleep on her own.

Jessica had been brilliant at sleeping in her cot but when she transferred to a bed, we had got into the habit of sitting with her until she fell asleep. It was fine until Steve started falling asleep with her only to wake an hour later feeling dreadful. The first night Steve sat on the floor, Jessica was hysterical but it turned out that that was the crucial change. We weathered that and then after three days of sitting further away Steve left her on her own and she has been fine ever since.

To make things easier, you could also try settling your child late, when she is really tired, and then gradually bring her bed-time forwards by 15 minutes each day until it reaches an acceptable time.

The crucial point is that you must not give in to your child. As in all behaviour management if you let your child cry for an hour and then give in to her, you will have taught her that if she cries enough she will get what she wants. So then the next night she will cry for an hour confident that if she goes on long enough you will give in. You want to teach her the opposite – that you are resolute and she will do better to co-operate.

If your child is crying and you find it disturbing, go and find something to do which will distract you, even if it is just the washing up with the radio on.

WAKING IN THE NIGHT

Usually children who wake in the night and need to be resettled are those who are unable to fall asleep on their own in their own bed. If you have successfully solved the problem of settling, you will probably also solve the problem of waking in the night. All children, however, may be disturbed by nightmares, coughs, itchiness or other illnesses from time to time but you should be able to go to their room, reassure them and leave promptly.

If your child continues to wake in the night you should think about the rewards you may be giving her intentionally or unintentionally. It might be a kiss and a stroke, a drink, a cuddle, a visit to your bed or even games. You must stop those rewards. Once your child realizes that she is not going to gain anything by waking up in the night she will stop. There are two approaches to stopping rewards:

1. Stop all rewards immediately. If she wakes, put her to bed, tell her to 'go to sleep', give no eye contact and just check every five minutes that all is okay.

2. Alternatively gradually reduce the rewards until she is going back to sleep on her own. For instance, if she is used to a cuddle you could give a very quick cuddle and then put her down, gradually reducing the cuddling over time until it is just a kiss or a pat and then nothing. If she is used to a drink of milk, give water instead and then nothing.

We tried the gradual approach with Ethan who at eight months had got so used to having a nice breastfeed and cuddle in the night that he continued to wake up even though he was not really hungry. One night we offered him a drink of water instead but he was not interested at all so then we just left him to cry and checked on him occasionally. Within a few days he was sleeping through the night.

GETTING INTO PARENTS' BED

Children love getting into their parents' bed for a cuddle and play before they get up in the morning. If you are happy for your children to do that then all is fine. However, you do not want them sleeping in your bed even for a short time if you want to establish a good sleep routine.

If your child gets into bed with you in the middle of the night then you should take her straight back to her own bed with the minimum of fuss and eye contact and keep repeating this for as long as it takes for her to give up and go to sleep.

Some children can be extraordinarily quiet and can get into your bed in the middle of the night without you even realizing it. If your child does this often you can devise something to alert you, a bell on a closed door, for example, and then take her straight back to bed.

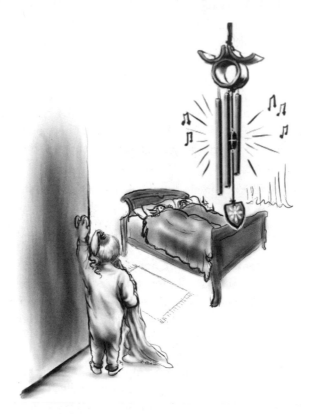

Devise something to alert you

CHILDREN WHO WAKE TOO EARLY

If your child wakes too early you should try to ignore her, perhaps leaving her until a little bit later each day until you reach a time that is acceptable to you. You can put some interesting and special toys in her room and place a stair-gate across the entrance so that she cannot get out. Additionally, if your child has the understanding, have a radio, alarm or light which, when it comes on, is the signal that it is okay to get up. In the summer when it is light very early, children can be woken by the light and think it is time to get up. You can try blacking out the window with extra sheeting or curtain lining.

DAYTIME NAPS

Some children, like adults, find that a daytime sleep gives them enough of an energy boost that they do not go to sleep at bed-time. Others are the opposite and find it difficult to sleep if they are too tired. Observe your child's patterns and see whether she sleeps better with or without a daytime nap. If she sleeps better with a nap, plan one into your daily routine. If, on the other hand, a nap keeps her up late, try to avoid giving her opportunities to fall asleep such as watching television or taking long drives in the late afternoon.

GOOD BEGINNINGS

If you have a very young baby who still needs to feed in the night, you can still start establishing good practice by making sure that at least sometimes she is put in her cot awake and left to fall asleep on her own and that you go to her at night rather than bring her into your bed.

OTHER POINTS

- If your child is ill, forget about good sleep practice and just wait till she is fully recovered before starting again.

- If you are following the above approach without success, it may be because you are not identifying your child's reward for waking up. Think very carefully about what your child is getting out of waking up.

- Some families find themselves gradually developing extraordinary routines in order to get their children to sleep. If you find yourself in this situation, you will probably need to talk to a professional to help you change your approach.

- If you have fears and anxieties about your child, they are much more likely to surface at night time and they may stop you from feeling able to leave your child at night. You may need help to address those issues before you can deal with sleep problems.

Toilet training

When your child is showing some awareness that she is weeing or pooing in her nappy, is doing proper wees rather than continual dribbles and perhaps showing some interest in using the potty or toilet, start to think about toilet training.

Toilet training is one of the most emotive areas of child development. Do not get upset about it. There is a huge variation in the ages when ordinary children are ready for potty training, let alone children with special needs. Other parents will talk about their own child's successes and you may feel pressure to start toilet training, particularly from people of the older generation who tried to potty train earlier. Ignore them and think only of your child, her needs and development stage.

As well as your child being ready you must think of your own needs:

- Think about what toilet training will mean for you. Changing nappies is one thing but clearing up soiled pants and mopping up puddles can really get you down. You must not show any annoyance with your child and it can be quite difficult. Make sure you are in a mood to handle it.

- Try it at a settled time when there are no major emotional disruptions such as a new baby or a trip away. It will be easier for you and your child.

- It is much easier to potty train in your own home, when you are not out and about too much and haven't got to worry about other people's expensive carpets.

Preparations and practical arrangements

Make life as easy as possible for everyone:

- There will be a lot of washing and a lot of clearing up. Summer is therefore easier because washing dries quicker, children wear less and you can do a lot of potty training outside.

- Make sure your child is wearing clothes which are easy to remove, like pull-on trousers rather than dungarees.

- Buy lots of pairs of pants as you will get through masses each day to begin with.

- A period when your child is on holiday from playgroup is often a good time to start as you can stay at home more easily and get people to come to you. If your child goes to a playgroup, school or childminder keep them informed and get them to use the same method.

- Use either a potty or a training seat, whatever suits your child. To begin with take it everywhere with you as your child will probably not be able to give you much warning. For example, have a potty downstairs, upstairs and in the car or pushchair when you go out. Specialist equipment is available from occupational therapists if you need it.

The theory

Once you start you should not stop but persist, however long it takes. However, if you find you have misjudged the timing and your child is clearly not ready, stop, go back to nappies and try again in three to six months time.

YOU MUST PRAISE SUCCESSES TO THE SKIES AND IGNORE FAILURES
Be as relaxed as possible. It is important not to get cross or to show any kind of annoyance or frustration at having to clear up mess because it can be counter-productive, making your child upset and unco-operative.

You need a word, sign or symbol to indicate 'toilet'. It might be a photograph or line drawing of a toilet, the word toilet or wee, or you could use the Makaton sign or your own personal sign or word. Eventually you will want it to be generally understood. If your child does not yet understand the symbol, sign or word you will need to give her one. Every time she goes on the potty or toilet show the symbol, make the sign or say the word and keep reinforcing it. Make sure other people who care for her know what her sign or word for toilet is.

> My son used the sign for horse because we live in the New Forest and there is a lot of horse dung around so he made an association between horse and poo! After a few months he picked up the proper sign for toilet.

BE PATIENT
It may take days, weeks or months. However long it takes there may be lapses for a long time afterwards. Changes of routine, too much excitement, illness, different drinks and different environments can make toilet training go to pot (if you will excuse the pun) for a few hours or days.

The practice

Show your child what to do. Take her to the toilet with you and show her your wee and poo. You can even use the potty yourself for a bit.

Put your child on the potty when you think you might have some success. For instance, if you know she always does a poo after lunch, take her nappy off and put her on the potty then. See what success you have.

At some point, however, you will have to take the plunge, stop using nappies altogether and put your child on the potty, either when you think you might have some success or very frequently (maybe every half an hour to begin with).

Ignore accidents totally and don't get upset if she doesn't do anything on the potty. When your child does do something in the potty praise her excessively, if possible get the whole family to admire her achievements. Really overdo the praise with smiles, clapping, shouting etc.

As a parent you may be able to recognize that your child wants to go to the loo by her body language such as scratching the groin or manic behaviour. Use those clues.

That's all there is to it. You just want to catch some poo or wee, praise or reward her and the praise will encourage your child to repeat her achievement when she is placed on the potty.

Initially you will control when your child goes on the potty. It is a nuisance for you to be forever remembering to put her on the potty but it is also a pain for your child, so she will learn to say 'no' when you suggest it and she is not interested.

> My son used to pull his trousers straight back up again and then learnt vehement head shaking as a response to 'Do you want the potty?'

Eventually, your child will be able to tell you that she wants to use the toilet but initially she will only be able to give you short notice. Even if it's too late, never mind, just praise her for telling you. Gradually she will recognize her needs more easily and give you more notice. Carry a potty with you everywhere and don't be embarrassed about getting it out and using it in public. It is a lot easier than dealing with a child who has wet or soiled pants.

POINTS TO REMEMBER

- Sometimes it can be very difficult to get a child to sit on the potty at all. Try entertaining her with something she loves – reading books, singing games or blowing bubbles – to get her on the potty and to keep her there for a few minutes.

- When you start potty training it is tempting to put nappies back on when you go out, but ultimately you have to make the commitment to toilet training and remove them totally. It is too confusing for a child to work out that when she has nappies on she can wee in her nappy but when she hasn't she must wee in the potty.

- If your child soils her pants make sure you clean the poo into the potty to reinforce that the 'poo goes in the potty not your pants'.

- Watch out that you don't make a reward out of failure. Some children love seeing all the fuss involved with clearing up the mess. If that is the case, exclude your child from the scene as quickly as you can without upsetting her and then clean up.

- Some children learn to wee in the potty first, some to poo first and some to do both simultaneously. There is no right or wrong order. There is nothing you can do but be patient.

- If your child's toilet training seems to be going backwards increase the level of praise again to regain momentum. It could be that you have got out of the habit of praising success.

DRY AT NIGHT

There is not much you can do to make your child dry at night except wait for her to do it by herself. If you notice her nappy is dry consistently in the mornings remove nappies at night and see what happens. Try the following ideas to establish a good routine or if things start going wrong:

- Put your child on the potty last thing at night and first thing in the morning.

- If she wets her bed at around waking up time, set your alarm for 30 minutes earlier than normal and get her up to wee in the potty to re-establish the routine. Once dry again gradually move the alarm setting back.

- Leave a potty in her bedroom so she can easily get up to use it.

- In the winter when it is very dark your child may not want to get up to use the toilet. Leave a low wattage light on somewhere useful so that she can see her way to the toilet confidently.

- Use mattress liners and half sheets to ease changing wet sheets in the middle of the night.

- Use star charts and other rewards if your child has the necessary level of understanding.

CHAPTER 10

The Support Your Child Should Expect

Support from health, education and social services

This section lists the different professionals, services and places you may come across in your child's early years. There is a national policy to ensure that children receive the services they need and that professionals communicate with each other whilst providing flexible services which meet the needs of the child and family. How this is interpreted and delivered will vary according to where you live and you may still have to push to find out about services and get the level of provision that you think your child needs. Local organizations and networks of parents are probably the best way of finding out what is available in your area.

Birth – 2 years

In your child's early years you will probably be caring for him mainly in the home with visits to and from professionals but you may have access to Opportunity Groups or therapy groups. Listed below are some of the professionals, services and places you may encounter.

PROFESSIONALS
General practitioner (GP)
GPs are often the first point of contact for parents with concerns about their child's health and development. They will refer children on to more specialist services as necessary. They provide ongoing support and should be an advocate for your child ensuring he gets the services he needs.

Health visitor
All children have a health visitor through their GP surgery. Health visitors have a role identifying children who are not meeting their milestones and signposting them to the right services. Checks will vary according to where you live, but usually a GP will carry out a six-week check and a health visitor will carry out an assessment before the child's first birthday. Health visitors are always available for parents if they have concerns about health or child care issues like feeding, behaviour and sleep.

Occupational therapist (OT)
OTs are concerned with fine motor and gross motor skills, seating and positioning, toileting, feeding, dressing, sensory integration and perceptual skills.

They work with parents to establish a programme of activities which parents can work on and they provide equipment for feeding or seating to aid the child's development. The frequency with which an OT will see your child can vary from weekly appointments to an occasional visit to address a specific problem.

OTs work with children in their homes, early years settings and school, but there should always be liaison with parents.

Paediatrician
The paediatrician is a doctor who specializes in children's health. He or she has an overall responsibility for your child's development and should ensure that he gets the support and services he needs.

Physiotherapist
Physiotherapists are concerned with physical development. They are always concerned with gross motor movements and sometimes with fine motor skills too.

They work on physical activities with the child and give parents a programme of activities for them to work on. Some children may need regular physiotherapy for many years, some may need an intensive period only and others may be seen only occasionally.

Pre-school children can be seen at home, in early years settings or at school, but parents should always be involved.

Social worker
Social workers can provide support for parents ensuring they get the information, support and services they need, for instance respite care, help in the home, counselling and equipment. If a family uses any of the services they should have a full assessment of their needs made but often this is not deemed necessary and it does not guarantee any services. Recently direct payments have been introduced, which give parents the funding to arrange and pay for their own services.

Specialist teacher adviser
Specialist teacher advisers provide support, help, advice and ideas on games, activities and practical issues for parents of children who are visually or hearing impaired or have a physical disability. They will visit homes and schools.

Speech and language therapist
Speech and language therapists work with children to help their communication skills and sometimes their feeding skills. They assess a child and draw up a programme of activities for parents, schools or other staff to work on with the child on a regular basis.

WHEN DEALING WITH PROFESSIONALS
Always remember that you as a parent know your child far better than anyone else does. You must have the confidence and courage to make demands and decisions about your child. You know far better than any professional what your child's abilities are, where he has problems, where he needs help and when things are not working. The professionals are there to support and help you and your child but they are not the experts on him. Have confidence in your views and tell the professionals what you think because they want to know this. A true partnership between parent and professional will generate the best provision.

Try to create good relationships with professionals. Inevitably, you will get more help, advice and support and it will come much easier if you communicate well. Resources in most areas are constrained and therefore you often have to push, nag and fight for services, but you can do this while maintaining friendly relations.

If you are going to an important consultation with a professional, write down any questions you have before you go, because you may find you forget everything when you are on the spot. Also take someone along with you to help look after your child during the meeting. This will allow you to concentrate on talking to the professional and you can get the other person to help you remember what was said afterwards.

SERVICES
You may have access to one or more of the services described below.

Children and Adolescents Mental Health Service (CAMHS)
CAMHS is a multi-disciplinary service for children with emotional and behavioural difficulties. After an initial assessment, children are referred to the relevant professionals such as psychologists, social workers and play therapists.

Common Assessment Framework (CAF)
This system has been devised to try to improve outcomes for children. Children at risk of poor outcomes, perhaps because of a wide range of issues within the family, such as housing and mental health, as well as special needs, will have a CAF completed on them, which will enable a lead professional to ensure the child receives services from all necessary professionals, with minimal duplication and maximum co-ordination and information sharing.

Early Bird Programme
This is an early intervention programme for pre-school children with a diagnosis of Autism Spectrum Disorder. Through a series of workshops and home visits it enables parents to understand autism and consequent behaviour and to improve their child's communication skills. Contact the National Autistic Society for details of local programmes (see Chapter 11, Resources).

Early Support
This programme aims to ensure that services are co-ordinated and responsive to the needs of families of children with complex difficulties aged 0–5. The Early Support Programme (ESP) Co-ordinator meets families and they mutually agree a Keyworker who will support the

family in the care of their child and liaise with all the professionals to make sure information is shared between them and that services are joined up. The Keyworker provides a range of excellent materials and resources on benefits, different disabilities and development journals. The Keyworker is someone already known by the family, for example a portage worker or teacher adviser. There are six-monthly multi-agency reviews of the child's progress, at which parents can help set the agenda.

To be eligible a child must be seeing a paediatrician and two other professionals. See the website www.earlysupport.org.uk for further information.

Holiday play schemes

Some social services departments and voluntary organizations run play schemes for children with special needs during the holidays. These provide both enjoyable and educational experiences for children and respite for parents. Contact social services or enquire locally to find out what is available in your area.

Opportunity Group

These are pre-schools for children with special needs, sometimes also their siblings and other children. They vary in the way they are run. Some have no staff but provide an opportunity for parents to bring their children together to play. Others have paid or voluntary staff who provide one on one support for the children and will work on programmes such as portage, OT and physiotherapy and give parents respite. Some have input directly from professionals. They are usually run by a voluntary committee of parents.

Portage

Portage is a home-based scheme for pre-school children which is based on a partnership with parents. A portage home visitor visits your home on a weekly or fortnightly basis for about an hour to observe your child, introduce new skills and ensure new achievements are generalized through play involving parents and other family members. Every six months, the parents and home visitor decide on a list of goals for your child and will then work towards achieving them. Each week the home visitor draws up an activity chart and the parents carry out a specified activity each day and record the child's response on the chart. Progress is very carefully monitored. To be eligible a child usually has to have problems in more than one area of development.

Respite care
Many parents feel the need for respite care so that they can have a break from caring for their child or spend some time with their other children or partner. Respite care is offered under a number of schemes and can vary from a few hours per week or month, to overnight stays, weekend breaks and extra help in school holidays. Unfortunately eligibility criteria and the availability of carers and funding can be highly variable. Contact your local Social or Children's Services for further information on the schemes available to you. Some social services departments make a charge. Alternatively, you may be able to use direct payments, a scheme whereby you receive the funding and then recruit and pay for your own carers and you can organize the care to suit your family.

PLACES
Child development centre
Some health authorities run child development centres which children with special needs attend. All the therapists and the paediatrician attend regularly. Children may attend just for a short assessment period or for a longer duration.

Children's Centres
These are being developed throughout the country, but the services they provide will vary according to local need. They should always be able to direct you to the services and professionals you require even if they do not offer them on site.

3 + Pre-school years

Children in all pre-schools and nurseries follow the Early Years Foundation Stage which sets out areas of development and learning for children under five. It is based on children learning through play and exploration.

CHOOSING A PRE-SCHOOL
From the age of three children are entitled to attend a nursery, playgroup or pre-school (hereafter called pre-school). Under the Disability

Discrimination Act, pre-schools cannot discriminate against disabled children and all pre-schools should make the necessary arrangements to ensure that all children can attend and thrive in their local mainstream provision. However, you may think a specialist group within a Children's Centre or special school more appropriate or choose to send your child to both a mainstream and specialist setting, spending a few sessions in each.

There is usually a range of different pre-schools within communities. It is worth visiting a number of them to see how they operate, what the atmosphere is like and what approach they adopt, how they treat your child and how much experience they have. Then you can decide which one would best meet your child's needs. Perhaps the most important element is whether they demonstrate a real commitment to making their provision work for your child.

Consider all your child's needs, perhaps using the major chapter headings of this book (physical, cognitive etc.) as a structure to help you consider what his developmental needs are and how they can best be met.

Mainstream pre-schools

Each pre-school must operate within the Special Educational Needs Code of Practice and have a Special Educational Needs Co-ordinator (SENCO) who is responsible for ensuring that the group meets the needs of disabled children. The SENCO should discuss your child's needs and find the extra support, help and equipment needed and identify information, training and advice as necessary.

If a child provides cause for concern, they may need some extra support from within the group such as extra staff for certain tasks or a visual timetable. This help is called Early Years Action and would probably include an Individual Education Plan (IEP) outlining short-term goals for your child.

If your child is not making enough progress with this support, the SENCO might need external help, for example from a speech therapist or specialist teacher adviser, and this level of support would be called Early Years Action Plus.

If it is clear that a child will struggle when he moves on to primary school, the Area Inclusion Co-ordinator (see below) will bring in an educational psychologist to assess the child and set a statutory assessment in motion so that a statement is in place when he starts school. See below for further details.

If pre-schools require extra help and expertise to address your child's needs they can call on support from the following professionals and services:

Outreach workers
Portage and special schools often have outreach workers who can give support and advice to pre-schools.

Area Inclusion Co-ordinators (INCO)
They support the SENCOs and pre-schools by giving training on SEN and statutory assessments. They can also support individual children with parental consent. They can provide funding for extra staff and equipment if needed for a child.

Specialist teacher advisers
See p.225 for details.

Specialist nurseries
Some special schools or children's centres have nursery classes for children with special needs. Children who attend these will have had their needs identified by professionals early on. They will probably be in the process of receiving or may already have received a statement of Special Educational Needs. Specialist nurseries will have access to the range of professionals outlined above.

4+ School age

When children enter school, at the age of four, they will continue to follow the Early Years Foundation Stage curriculum.

SELECTING A SCHOOL

Most children with special needs attend mainstream primary school but parents do have a choice of mainstream, special school or a resourced unit.

It is worth visiting all possible schools with an open mind. Try to think what would suit your child at that particular time and try not to be too prejudiced for or against one particular form of education. You need to work out in which environment your child would thrive and where his needs would be best met by considering the issues below:

- local versus non-local (part of the local community, distance to travel)
- integration versus segregation (learning alongside 'normal' children, role models, teasing)
- experienced staff versus general classroom teachers (specialist experience, training in special needs, role of teaching assistants)
- access to therapists (physio, occupational therapists etc.)
- facilities (access to hydrotherapy, sensory rooms)
- curriculum (development level, appropriateness of the curriculum, structure, how they meet child's individual needs).

TRANSITION TO SCHOOL

The pre-school will hold meetings with relevant schools and pass on information about children so that the new teachers have the benefit of the pre-school's experience and knowledge of the individual needs of the children.

It is important to manage the transition from one setting to the next carefully, ensuring that information is passed on to the new setting, children are prepared for the change, roles and responsibilities are clearly defined and appropriate targets are set. Your local authority may have an arrangement to manage this but, if not, it is worth requesting an informal plan for your child.

STATUTORY ASSESSMENT OR THE STATEMENTING PROCESS

If your child has special needs that are identified at pre-school, he may need to be assessed to ensure that when he starts school at four or five his special needs are properly identified and addressed by the teachers and school. This process is called the 'statutory assessment of special educational needs (SEN)'. Because it may result in a statement of special educational needs it is often called 'statementing'.

If your child is already at school and his teachers have identified that he has special educational needs, he would normally go through a number of stages aimed at addressing his needs within the school before requesting a statement. Initially, the school can get additional or different help from within the school for example one-to-one help – this is called School Action. If this is insufficient, then the school could bring in outside specialists such as an educational psychologist – this is called School Action Plus. Only if these were not sufficient for your child to make satisfactory progress would a statutory assessment be requested.

Statementing is a very complex, detailed and lengthy process that is carried out by your local authority (LA) Children's Services Department. The aim is to identify your child's particular needs for education, for example a specific number of hours of extra support or a programme of speech therapy delivered by school staff but supervised by a speech therapist. Only a small proportion of children will have needs that require a statement. The majority of children with special educational needs will be supported through School Action and School Action Plus in a mainstream school.

As a parent, you have two main responsibilities:

1.   To give as much detailed information about your child as you can, so that the LA can make an informed judgement.

2.   To consider all schools that might be appropriate, and decide which you think would be best for your child.

The procedure
You can apply for a statutory assessment at any time as long as no assessment has been undertaken in the previous six months. A statutory assessment is unusual for a child under two but if requested the LA must undertake such an assessment. LA and health authorities should liaise to identify pre-school children who may require an assessment prior to school entry and therefore an assessment would usually be made as a child is approaching school age.

There is an initial form to complete in which you should give a brief description of your child, his educational progress and the professionals involved. From this and other information and evidence the LA will decide if there are sufficient grounds to proceed with a statutory assessment.

If the LA decides to proceed they gather reports from all the professionals involved with your child (for example teachers, educational psychologists, paediatricians, occupational therapists and portage). You are requested to provide an assessment of your child's development and give your views on his educational needs.

The LA will then consider all the reports it receives and may draw up a draft statement. This will give details of your child's special educational needs, the provision required to meet them, the long-term educational objectives and the non-educational needs and provision that he requires.

You should consider the content of the draft statement and request a meeting with the LA within two weeks if you are seeking clarification, changes or additions to the draft statement. Also at this stage you can make representations and/or express preferences for the school which you want your child to attend.

Once agreed the LA will then issue the final statement which will state the school your child will attend. The LA then has a statutory obligation to fulfil the requirements of the statement. If your child moves, the statement will go with him and the new LA will inherit the statutory obligations, but they do have the opportunity to request a revision.

A statement is reviewed at least annually involving parents and appropriate professional staff.

The LA may decide not to issue a statement because it has decided that your child can be supported adequately on School Action Plus or through a 'note in lieu of a statement' which outlines the support needed but does not have statutory status. If you disagree, you should talk to the LA and school. You can ask for an informal resolution or finally you can appeal to the Special Educational Needs and Disability Tribunal (SENDIST).

Time-scale
The time limit for undertaking a statutory assessment is 26 weeks but it may take a shorter or longer period depending on circumstances.

Appeal
There are rights of appeal for parents against decisions made by the LA.

Further information
The above is a very brief résumé of the statutory assessment process that may result in a statement for your child. For more detailed information request a free copy of 'Special Educational Needs: A Guide for Parents' and 'The Special Educational Needs Code of Practice', issued by the Department for Children, Schools and Families (Tel: 0845 6022260, email: dcfs@prolog.uk.com or download from http://publications.teachernet.gov.uk).

You can get further advice from the local Parent Partnership Service who are able to assist parents with the statutory assessment process and also provide parents with impartial advice, guidance and information. Contact your LA and ask for the Parent Partnership Service. Many voluntary organizations also produce useful guides to the statutory assessment. Contact organizations like Mencap, ACE and Network 81 or the voluntary organization specific to your own child's special needs, listed in Chapter 11, Resources.

Sources of support – finance and equipment

Having a child with special needs can lead to considerable extra costs, so I have listed below some of the sources of support available.

Social security benefits

There are various social security benefits you can claim for your child and for the main carer. These are in addition to child benefit which, as with all children, you are entitled to for each of your children. ·

Your local Citizens Advice Bureau can always advise you on your rights. Look in your telephone directory for their address and phone number.

DISABILITY LIVING ALLOWANCE (DLA)

This is an allowance for people or children who need help with personal care, with getting around or both. There are two components:

1. Care (for extra and additional care) available from birth (with a three month qualifying period) paid at three rates:
   - high – for people/children who need help both day and night
   - middle – for people/children who need help during the day or night
   - low – for people/children who need some help during the day.

2. Mobility (for help getting around) paid at two rates:
   - higher (from age three) – for people/children unable or virtually unable to walk
   - lower (from age five) – for people/children who need someone to provide them with guidance and supervision for most of the time they are outdoors in unfamiliar surroundings.

There is more information at www.direct.gov.uk/en/DisabledPeople/FinancialSupport.

The forms and accompanying literature can be off-putting and many parents find completing them very distressing. They have to demonstrate that their child requires a lot more care than an ordinary child. For most parents, who are just learning to cope with their situation, it is very disturbing to have to stress their child's difficulties in this way.

Nevertheless, fill in the forms with as much information as you can. If you feel that the questions are not very helpful add a statement of your own describing your child's needs at home and describing all the extra things you have to do – medical care, extra care for feeding and bathing, travelling time to appointments and pre-schools, extra washing, additional play, physiotherapy, OT, speech, portage programmes etc.

A Decision Maker at the Department for Work and Pensions will decide on whether you qualify and for which category – low, middle or high. You can ask for a reconsideration if you are not happy with the decision. You should write or call 08457 123456 to request it within one month and enclose any additional information. You should also ask for the Decision Maker's reasons in detail in writing at this stage and a copy of any medical evidence they have used. If you are still not happy with the decision you can go to appeal.

It is well worth giving as much information as possible to make your case and help the officials make their decision. It is also worth asking for a revision if you feel the decision has been unfair.

This significant benefit is not means tested, is not taxable and it may give you access to other benefits.

Contact the Benefit Enquiry Line on 0800 882200 for an application form. Or visit www.direct.gov.uk to claim online if you wish.

Your local Citizens Advice Bureau will give you advice on completing the forms and on any appeals. Your social worker should be able to help and many voluntary organizations like Cerebra and Contact a Family (see Chapter 11) give good advice and information.

CARER'S ALLOWANCE (CA)
This allowance is for those who are of working age and care for a child who gets Disability Living Allowance care component at the higher or middle rate. You must be caring for the child for at least 35 hours a week, not in full-time education and earning not more than £87 per

week after deduction of taxable allowances. The allowance is taxable. The application form is very straightforward.

To obtain a form contact the Benefit Enquiry Line on 0800 882200 or visit www.direct.gov.uk.

If you have other people to support, e.g. children or a partner, you may be able to get more than the basic rate, but it depends on other earnings and benefits you may be getting.

If you receive income support you can claim CA with an extra carer's premium but your income support will be reduced by the basic amount of the CA.

If you receive CA you automatically get credited with national insurance contributions so that your pension is protected.

TAX CREDITS

These are dependent on income and vary according to several factors such as the number of children in the family and hours worked per week.

Child Tax Credit

This can be claimed by anyone with a dependent child, whether working or not. There is a family element with amounts for each child. There are increased amounts if the child has a disability.

Working Tax Credit

This can be claimed by anyone with a child, who is working or whose partner is working for at least 16 hours per week. It can sometimes help towards child care costs.

For application forms contact Tax Credit Helpline on 0845 3003900

COUNCIL TAX REDUCTIONS

If you have made major alterations to your house for your child's benefit you may be eligible for a band reduction on your council tax. Contact your local authority for more details.

ADDITIONAL FINANCIAL SUPPORT

There are many local charities, such as the Rotary Club and Lions Club, which may be able to give financial support or you could contact the following national organizations:

Family Fund Trust
Unit 4, Alpha Court
Monks Cross Drive, Huntington
York YO32 9WN
Tel: 0845 1304542
Email: info@familyfund.org.uk
Website: www.familyfundtrust.org.uk

Provides grants for families of very severely disabled children aged 15 or under based on the families' views and needs. Gives financial grants which relate directly to the child's needs, e.g. for help with play equipment, extra laundry, getting around, holidays or outings. Assistance can only be given to those families whose gross income is less than £23,000 and have no more than £18,000 in savings (2007 figures). For more information and an application form contact the above address or see the website.

Family Welfare Association
501–505 Kingsland Road
Dalston
London E8 4AU
Tel: 020 72546251
Email: grants.enquiry@fwa.org.uk
Website: www.fwa.org.uk

Can provide one-off grants to people and families who are living on low incomes, particularly those living on benefit. Money can be given for a range of needs such as clothing, fuel bills and household items. It can also help with more varied needs such as school uniform. Council tax, rent arrears, fines etc. cannot be covered. Grants are usually between £100 and £200. Applications are made through a health visitor, social worker or Citizens Advice Bureau.

OTHER SUPPORT
Blue badge scheme
You can apply for a blue badge which allows you to park in disabled parking spaces or on yellow lines if you are out with your child. Your child must be over two years old and in receipt of the higher mobility rate of DLA or must be registered blind. Contact your local County Council or Social Services if you think you are eligible.

Free nappies

If your child is still in nappies at four years old you can apply for free nappies from your local health authority. Contact your health visitor for an assessment.

Pushchairs

You may be able to have the loan of a single or double pushchair or vouchers towards buying one, if your child still needs one when he is two years and six months. Contact your health visitor, GP or occupational therapist for an assessment.

Adaptations to houses

Local authorities have powers to make grants for alterations to houses to adapt them for disabled people and children over the age of three. The rules are complex, so contact your local authority for details.

Motability

City Gate House, 22 Southwark Bridge Road
London SE1 9HB
Tel: 0845 4564566
Website: www.motability.co.uk

Motability, which is a non-profit making organization, runs a scheme to enable those in receipt of the higher rate Mobility Component of Disability Living Allowance to lease or buy a car. They operate schemes which help those who need to pay for adaptations to cars including the Government's grant scheme (Mobility Equipment Fund). To qualify for the higher rate Mobility Component of DLA a child must be over three years old (see p.234). Motability also operate a hire purchase scheme for wheelchairs.

CHAPTER 11

Resources

Bibliography
Attention Deficit Disorder (ADD)

Flick, G.L. (1998) ADD/ADHD Behaviour Change Resource Kit: Ready to Use Strategies and Activities for Helping Children with ADD. New York: Center for Applied Research in Education.

Jones, C.B. (1991) Sourcebook for Children with ADD. San Antonio, TX: Communication Skill Builders.

Autism

Attwood, T. (1993) Why Does Chris Do That? London: National Autistic Society.

Baron-Cohen, S. and Bolton, P. (1993) Autism: The Facts. Oxford: Oxford University Press.

Beyer, J. and Gammetoft, L. (1999) Autism and Play. London: Jessica Kingsley Publishers.

Dickenson, P. and Hannah, L. (1998) It Can Get Better ... Dealing with Common Behavioural Problems in Young Autistic Children. London: National Autistic Society.

Ives, M. and Munro, N. (2002) Caring for a Child with Autism: A Practical Guide for Parents. London: Jessica Kingsley Publishers.

Moor, J. (2002) Playing, Laughing and Learning with Children on the Autism Spectrum. London: Jessica Kingsley Publishers.

Schopler, E. (ed.) (1995) Parent Survival Manual: A Guide to Crisis Resolution in Autism and Related Development Disorders. New York: Plenum Press.

Wing, L. (1996) The Autistic Spectrum: A Guide for Parents and Professionals. London: Constable and Co. Ltd.

Behaviour management

Lewis, P. (2005) Achieving Best Behaviour for Children with Developmental Disabilities: A Step by Step Work Book for Parents and Carers. London: Jessica Kingsley Publishers.

Pentecost, D. (2000) Parenting the ADD Child: Can't Do? Won't Do? Practical Strategies for Managing Behaviour Problems in Children with ADHD and ADD. London: Jessica Kingsley Publishers.

Phelan, T.W. (1995) 1–2–3 Magic: Effective Discipline for Children 2–12. Glen Ellyn, IL: Child Management Inc.

Cerebral palsy

Finnie, N.R. (1997) Handling the Young Child with Cerebral Palsy at Home. Oxford: Butterworth Heinemann.

Geralis, E. (ed.) (1998) Children With Cerebral Palsy. A Parent's Guide. Rockville, MD: Woodbine House.

Griffiths, M. and Clegg, M. (1988) Cerebral Palsy – Problems and Practice. London: Souvenir Press.

Martin, S. (2006) Teaching Motor Skills to Children with Cerebral Palsy and Similar Movement Disorders. Rockville, MD: Woodbine House.

Miller, F. and Bachrach, S.J. (2006) Cerebral Palsy – A Complete Guide to Caregiving. Baltimore: Johns Hopkins University Press.

Pimm, P. (2002) Living with Cerebral Palsy. London: Hodder and Wayland.

Stranton, M. (2002) The Cerebral Palsy Handbook. A Practical Handbook for Parents and Carers. London: Vermilion.

Child development

Lansdown, R. and Walker, M. (1997) Your Child's Development from Birth to Adolescence. London: Frances Lincoln Ltd.

Leach, P. (1974) Babyhood. London: Penguin.

Meggatt, C. (2006) Child Development an Illustrated Guide. Oxford: Heinemann.

Natanson, J. (1997) Learning Through Play. London: Ward Lock.

Sheridan, M.D. (1997) From Birth to Five Years, Children's Developmental Progress. London: Routledge.

Communication

Dyrbjerg, P. and Vedel, M. (2007) Everyday Education – Visual Support for Children with Autism. London: Jessica Kingsley Publishers.

Lynch, C. and Cooper, J. (1991) Early Communication Skills. Bicester, Oxon: Winslow.

Schwartz, S. (1996) The New Language of Toys: Teaching Communication Skills to Children with Special Needs. Rockville, MD: Woodbine House.

Shaw, C. (1993) Talking and Your Child. London: Hodder & Stoughton.

Sonders, S.A. (2002) Giggle Time: A Programme to Develop Communication Skills of Children with Autism. London: Jessica Kingsley Publishers.

Developmental Co-ordination Disorder/Dyspraxia

Boon, N. (2000) Helping Children with Dyspraxia. London: Jessica Kingsley Publishers.

Cocks, N. (1996) Watch Me I Can Do It: Helping Children Overcome Clumsy and Unco-ordinated Motor Skills. London: Simon & Schuster.

Kirby, A. (1999) Dyspraxia – The Hidden Handicap. London: Souvenir.

Penso, D. (1992) Perceptuo-Motor Difficulties: Theories and Strategies to Help Children, Adolescents and Adults. Cheltenham: Stanley Thorne.

Portwood, M (1999) Developmental Dyspraxia – Identification and Intervention: A Manual for Parents and Professionals. London: David Fulton.

Down's Syndrome

Bruni, M. (2006) Fine Motor Skills for Children with Down Syndrome: A Guide for Parents and Professionals. Rockville, MD: Woodbine House.

Buckley, S., Emslie, M. and Haslegrave, G. (1993) The Development of Language and Reading Skills in Children with Down's Syndrome. Portsmouth: University of Portsmouth.

Cunningham, C. (2006) Down's Syndrome: An Introduction for Parents. London: Souvenir Press.

Kumin, L. (2003) Communication Skills for Children with Down's Syndrome. Rockville, MD: Woodbine House.

Newton, R. (2003) Down's Syndrome Handbook. London: Vermilion.

Pueschel, S.M. (2000) A Parent's Guide to Down's Syndrome. Baltimore: Paul Brookes Publishing Co.

Routh, K. (2005) Down's Syndrome (Need to Know). Oxford: Heinemann.

Selikowitz, M. (1997) Down's Syndrome – The Facts. Oxford: Oxford University Press.

Winders, P.C. (1997) Gross Motor Skills in Children with Down Syndrome. Bethesda: Woodbine House.

Epilepsy

Freeman, J.M., Vining, E.P.G. and Pillas, D.J. (2003) Seizures and Epilepsy in Children: A Guide (3rd edn). Baltimore: Johns Hopkins University.

Kutscher, M.L. (2006) Children with Seizures: A Guide for Parents, Teachers and Other Professionals. London: Jessica Kingsley Publishers.

Reisner, H. (1988) Children with Epilepsy: A Parents Guide. Rockville MD: Woodbine House.

Hearing impaired

Marschark, M. (2007) Raising and Educating a Deaf Child. Oxford: Oxford University Press.

McCracken, W. and Sutherland, H. (1991) Deafability not Disability: Guide for Parents of Hearing Impaired Children. Clevedon: Multilingual Matters.

Medwid, D.J. and Chapman Weston, D. (1995) Kid-friendly Parenting with Deaf and Hard of Hearing Children. Washington, DC: Gallaudet University Press.

Schwartz, S. (2006) Choices in Deafness: A Parents' Guide to Communication Options (3rd edn). Rockville, MD: Woodbine House.

Smith, C. (1992) Signs Make Sense. London: Souvenir Press.

Life-limiting conditions

Brown, E. (2007) Supporting the Child and the Family in Paediatric Palliative Care. London: Jessica Kingsley Publishers.

Goldman, A., Hain, R. and Liben, S. (eds) (2006) Oxford Textbook of Palliative Care for Children. Oxford: Oxford University Press.

Cook, P. (1999) Supporting Sick Children and their Families. London: Bailliere Tindall.

Play ideas

Denziloe, J. (1994) Fun and Games: Practical Leisure Ideas for People with Profound Disabilities. Oxford: Butterworth Heinemann.

Gee, R. and Meredith, S. (1993) Entertaining and Educating your Preschool Child. London: Usborne.

Lear, R. (1996) Play Helps. Oxford: Butterworth Heinemann.

Lear, R. (1998) Look at It This Way: Toys and Activities for Children with a Visual Impairment. Oxford: Butterworth Heinemann.

Lear, R. (1999) Fingers and Thumbs: Toys and Activities for Children with Hand Problems. Oxford: Heinemann Butterworth.

Lear, R. (2001) Fun Without Fatigue: Toys and Activities for Children with Restricted Movement. Oxford: Heinemann Butterworth.

Morris, L.R. and Shultz, L. (1989) Creative Play Activities for Children with Disabilities. Champaign, IL: Human Kinetics Books.

National Association of Toy and Leisure Libraries (1990) Switch Play into Action. London: NATLL.

Rice, M. (1993) Child's Play. London: Kingfisher Books.

Streeter, E. (1993) Making Music with the Young Child with Special Needs. London: Jessica Kingsley Publishers.

Sensory integration disorder

Anderson, E. and Emmons, P. (2005) Understanding Sensory Dysfunction. London: Jessica Kingsley Publishers.

Cribbin, V., Lynch, H., Bagshawe, B. and Chadwick, K. (2003) Sensory Integration Information Booklet. Blackrock, Co. Dublin: Sensory Integration Network, UK.

Inamura, L.M. (1998) SI for Early Intervention, a Team Approach. Texas: Therapy Skill Builders.

Kranowitz, C.S. (2007) The Out of Sync Child: Recognizing and Coping with Sensory Integration Dysfunction. New York: Skylight Press.

Williams, M.S. and Schellenberger, S. (1994) How Does Your Engine Run? A Leaders Guide to the Alert Programme for Self-Regulation. Alberquerque, NM: TherapyWorks Inc.

Siblings

Harries, A. and McCaffrey, M. (2005) Special Brothers and Sisters. London: Jessica Kingsley Publishers.

Powell, T.P. and Gallagher, P.A. (1996) Brothers and Sisters: A Special Part of Exceptional Families. Baltimore: Paul H. Brookes.

Sleep management

Durand, V.M. (1997) Sleep Better! A Guide to Improving Sleep for Children with Special Needs. Baltimore: Paul H. Brookes.

Ferber, R. (2002) Solve your Child's Sleep Problems: A Practical and Comprehensive Guide for Parents. London: Dorling Kindersley.

Special needs

Bartram, P. (2007) Understanding your Young Child with Special Needs. London: Jessica Kingsley Publishers.

Greenspan, S.I. and Wieder, S. with Simons, R. (1998) The Child with Special Needs: Encouraging Intellectual and Emotional Growth. Reading, MA: Merloyd Lawrence.

Gill, G. (1997) Changed by a Child: Companion Notes for a Child with a Disability. New York: Broadway Books.

Hannaford, C. (1995) Smart Moves: Why Learning is Not All in Your Head. Arlington: Great Ocean Publishers.

Knight, A. (1996) Caring for a Disabled Child. London: Straightforward Publishing.

Woolfson, R. (1991) Children with Special Needs. London: Faber & Faber Ltd.

Visually impaired

Sonksen, P. and Stiff, B. (2001) Show Me What My Friends Can See: A Developmental Guide for Babies with Severely Impaired Sight and their Professional Advisers. London: Institute of Child Health.

RNIB (2001) Play it My Way: Learning Through Play with your Visually Impaired Child. London: RNIB E&E.

Coleman, M. (2001) Play It Right: Creating and Adapting Toys and Games for Children who are Visually Impaired and Have Additional Needs. London: RNIB E&E.

Voluntary organizations offering support for parents of children with special needs

Listed below are national organizations which provide support and information for parents of children with special needs who are of pre-school age or just starting school. Both mainstream and alternative organizations are listed. I have focused on the services provided which are relevant to the pre-school age group rather than trying to describe everything in full. Contact the organizations directly to request full details of what they do and find out about other related organizations.

There are also many excellent local charities and support groups which it is not practical to list here.

Most organizations provide information to parents free of charge, even if they are not members. However, since membership costs are usually fairly nominal, it is often well worth joining the organization relevant to your child. Many have comprehensive mail order book catalogues and so are a good source of relevant books.

If your child has a disability not included in the lists consult 'The CaF Directory of Specific Conditions and Rare Syndromes in Children with their Family Support Networks' (most public libraries have a copy) which lists many more organizations.

National organizations

The organizations below are listed alphabetically.

Action for Sick Children
The National Children's Bureau
8 Wakley St
London EC1V 7QE
Tel: 01663 763870
Helpline: 0800 074 4519
Email: enquiries@actionforsickchildren.org
Website: www.actionforsickchildren.org

Aims to raise standards of healthcare for all children whether at home or in hospital. Provides support and advice for parents with sick children through a national network and produces publications on 'When your Child is Sick', 'Coming into Hospital' and 'Children and Pain'. Campaigns to enable parents to have a greater role in their children's hospital care.

Advisory Centre for Education
Unit 1C Aberdeen Studios
22–24 Highbury Grove
London N5 2DQ
Tel: 020 7704 3370
Advice line: 0808 800 5793 (10–5, Monday–Friday)
Website: www.ace-ed.org.uk

Believes that children benefit from greater openness and accountability in education. Therefore encourages parents to become actively involved in their child's education. Produces a range of publications on school and education including 'Special Education Handbook: The Law on Children with Special Needs'.

Arthritis Care
18 Stephenson Way
London NW1 2HD
Helpline: 0808 800 4050
Email: helplines@arthritiscare.org.uk
Website: www.arthritiscare.org.uk

Provides information and advice on a range of issues related to living with arthritis. Campaigns locally and nationally to make sure people with arthritis have access to the treatments and services they need.

AFASIC (Association for All Speech Impaired Children)
2nd Floor
50–52 Great Sutton Street
London EC1V 0DJ
Helpline: 08453 55 55 77 (10.30–2.30, Monday–Friday)
Tel: 020 7490 9410 (admin)
Email: info@afasic.org.uk
Website: www.afasic.org.uk

Represents children with communication impairments, works for their inclusion in society and supports their parents and carers. Provides a helpline, training conferences and publications and support through local groups.

Association for Spina Bifida and Hydrocephalus
ASBAH House
42 Park Road
Peterborough PE1 2UQ
Tel: 01733 555988
Helpline: 0845 450 7755
Email: info@asbah.demon.co.uk
Website: www.asbah.org

For individuals with spina bifida and/or hydrocephalus and their families. Provides advice, advocacy, information and other services. Publishes a quarterly magazine plus pamphlets, notably an information pack for new parents which covers such issues as developing skills through toys, positioning and exercises and statementing. Advisers will give individual advice to families concerning continence, education, mobility, benefits and medical issues.

The Bobath Centre for Children with Cerebal Palsy
250 East End Road
London N2 8AU
Tel: 020 8444 3355
Email: info@bobathlondon.co.uk
Website: www.bobathlondon.co.uk

Specifically for children with cerebal palsy. Aims to encourage and increase the child's ability to move and function as normally as possible using the Bobath technique which the centre has developed.

Brainwave Centre
Huntworth Gate
Bridgewater
Somerset TA6 6LQ
Tel: 01278 429089
Email: enquiries@brainwave.org.uk
Website: www.brainwave.org.uk

For brain-injured children aged 6 months to 12 years. Designs individual tailored programmes of therapy which are carried out at home with help from family and volunteers for up to 12 hours per week.

Breakthrough Trust – Deaf Hearing Integration
Alan Geale House
The Close
Westhill Campus
Bristol Road
Selly Oak
Birmingham B29 6LN
Tel: (minicom and voice) 0121 472 6447

For deaf and hearing people who want to come together in the spirit of integration and understanding through training, social activities and contact groups. Offers courses using new technology for communication, family contact groups and after-school clubs.

British Deaf Association
BDA Midlands
Coventry Point, 10th Floor
Market Way
Coventry CV1 1EA
Tel: 0247 655 0936
Text: 0247 655 0393
Website: www.bda.org.uk

Promotes deaf people as equal partners in society and campaigns for the deaf community to be accepted as an integral part of British life with British Sign Language seen as an accepted minority language. Offers services in the following areas: education and youth, information and media access, advocacy, development in the community and health promotion. Members receive a regular newsletter with information on services and campaigns.

The British Institute for Brain Injured Children
Knowle Hall
Bridgewater
Somerset TA7 8PJ
Tel: 01278 684060

Email: info@bibic.org.uk
Website: www.bibic.org.uk
www.myspace.com/bibic_org_uk

Teaches parents of brain-injured children stimulation therapy which they can practise at home after assessment.

British Institute of Learning Difficulties
Campion House
Green Street
Kidderminster
Worcs DY10 1JH
Tel: 01562 723010
Email: enquiries@bild.org.uk

For anyone working with people with a learning disability. Publishes books and various journals, including the 'British Journal of Learning Disabilities', and also provides training.

British Society for Music Therapy
61 Church Hill Road
East Barnet
Herts EN4 8SY
Tel: 020 8441 6226
Website: www.bsmt.org

For all those with an interest in music therapy. Holds meetings, workshops and conferences, produces journals and bulletins and has a comprehensive catalogue of books on all aspects of music therapy.

Brittle Bone Society
30 Guthrie Street
Dundee DD1 5BS
Tel: 01382 204446
Helpline: 08000 28 24 59
Email: bbs@brittlebone.org
Website: www.brittlebone.org

Provides information to anyone affected by brittle bones (Osteogenesis Imperfecta) and to those supporting them. Organizes local meetings and an annual conference. Works closely with doctors, occupational therapists, physiotherapists and nurses.

Carers UK
20–25 Glasshouse Yard
London EC1A 4JS
Tel: 020 7490 8818 (office)
Helpline: 0808 808 7777

Email: info@carersuk.org
Website: www.carersuk.org

Fights to end the ill health, poverty and discrimination faced by carers as a direct consequence of caring. Improves carers' lives by providing information and advice on carers' rights and campaigning for changes that make a real difference for carers.

Centre for Studies in Inclusive Education (CSIE)
New Redland Building
Coldharbour Lane
Frenchay
Bristol BS16 1QU
Tel: 0117 328 4007
Website: www.csie.org.uk

An independent education centre, supporting inclusion as a basic human right of every child. Works towards an end to segregated education. Produces publications (for example, 'The Index for Inclusion') and holds conferences, training and other events.

Cerebra
2nd Floor The Lyric Building
King Street
Carmarthen SA31 1BD
Tel: 01267 244 200
Parent Support Helpline: 0800 32 81 159
Email: info@cerebra.org.uk
Website: www.cerebra.org.uk

Offers information and services to the parents and carers of children with neurological condition. Provides a grant scheme; library offering sensory toys and books; wills and trusts and speech and language therapy schemes; holiday homes; personal portfolios and sleep service.

Child Brain Injury Trust (CBIT)
Unit 1 The Great Barn
Baynards Green Farm
Baynards Green
Bicester
Oxon OX27 7SG
Tel: 01869 341075
Helpline: 0845 601 4939 (10–1, Monday, Tuesday, Wednesday and Friday)
Email: info@cbituk.org
Website: www.cbituk.org

For children with acquired brain injury (i.e. not birth defects), their families and professionals. Provides advice, information on brain injury and special schools.

Supports research and has a hardship fund. Has outreach workers in Scotland, Northern Ireland and Newcastle.

Children's Legal Centre
University of Essex
Wivenhoe Park
Colchester
Essex CO4 3SQ
National Education Law Advice Line: 0845 345 4345
Child Law Advice Line: 0845 120 2948
Email: clc@essex.ac.uk

An independent national charity concerned with law and policy affecting children and young people. Staffed by legal specialists committed to protecting children's rights, helping children in need, parents and professionals. Offers free legal advice and representation for children and parents on family law and education law issues, advocacy for children and legal publications.

The Children's Trust
Tadworth Court
Tadworth
Surrey KT20 5RU
Tel: 01737 365000

Provides care, education and therapy for children with multiple disabilities aged 0–19. Services include residential rehabilitation, community support, short breaks and palliative care.

Climb: Children Living with Inherited Metabolic Diseases
176 Nantwich Road
Crewe CW2 6BG
Freephone: 0800 652 3181
Tel: 0845 241 2172
Website: www.climb.org.uk

Provides information on over 700 metabolic conditions. Supports families and professionals through befrienders, family contacts and conferences.

Contact a Family
209–211 City Road
London EC1V 1JN
Tel: 020 7608 8700
Helpline: 0808 808 3555 (10–4, Mon–Fri, 5.30–7.30, Mon)
Email: info@cafamily.org.uk
Website: www.cafamily.org.uk

Provides advice, information and support to parents of all disabled children – no matter what their health condition. Enables parents to get in contact with other families through a family linking service, both on a local and national basis. Helpline offers advice on welfare, community care, education etc. Has local, regional offices plus volunteer family workers around the UK. Produces a range of publications including 'The Contact a Family Directory'.

Cystic Fibrosis Trust
11 London Road
Bromley
Kent BR1 1BY
Tel: 020 8464 7211
Helpline: 0845 859 1000
Website: www.cftrust.org.uk

For people with cystic fibrosis (CF), their families and professionals. Provides support for CF sufferers and their families including information, a magazine and notices of local meetings. Also funds research and clinics and raises awareness. Has a mail order list of publications on CF and physiotherapy, diet, financial help, school, genetics etc.

Deafblind UK
National Centre for Deafblindness
John and Lucille van Geest Place
Cygnet Road
Hampton
Peterborough PE7 8FD
Tel/Text: 01733 358100
Helpline: 0800 132320
Email: info@deafblind.org.uk
Website: www.deafblind.org.uk

Offers specialist services and support to people with combined sight and hearing loss. Aims to enable people to live independent and fulfilling lives. Provides practical support including communication and rehabilitaton training, volunteer befriending service, helpline, publications and adapted equipment for daily living.

DELTA: Deaf Education through Listening and Talking
The Con Powell Centre
3 Swan Court
Cygnet Park
Peterborough PE7 8GX
Tel: 0845 108 1437
Email: enquiries@deafeducation.org.uk
Website: www.deafeducation.org.uk

Promotes the natural aural approach, i.e. children are given hearing aids or cochlear implants to enhance what hearing they have and encouraged to develop spoken language by copying what they hear rather than using sign language. Helps families with severely or profoundly deaf children who want those children to acquire natural, effective spoken language. The aim is that deaf children will then have access to the hearing world. Provides workshops, meetings and summer schools, also a range of factsheets and booklets.

Disabled Living Foundation
380–384 Harrow Road
London W9 2HU
Tel: 020 7289 6111
Helpline: 0870 603 9177 (10–4, Monday–Friday)
Minicom: 0870 603 9176
Email: dlfinfo@dlf.org.uk
Website: www.dlf.org.uk

Provides information on equipment for disabled people. Offers a telephone helpline and responds to written enquiries. Has an equipment centre displaying equipment for people to try out. Also produces a range of publications on choosing and using equipment and on suppliers, e.g. 'Children's Play Equipment', 'Mobility Equipment' and 'Everyday Living Equipment'.

Down's Syndrome Association
Langdon Down Centre
2a Langdon Park
Teddington
Middlesex TW11 9PS
Tel: 0845 230 0372
Email: info@downs-syndrome.org.uk
Website: www.downs-syndrome.org.uk

Provides information and support to people with Downs's Syndrome, their families, carers and interested professionals. Produces a tri-annual journal and a range of literature about living with Down's Syndrome. Has a network of local parent support groups.

DownsEd: The Down Syndrome Educational Trust
The Sarah Duffen Centre
Belmont Street
Southsea
Portsmouth
Hants PO5 1NA
Tel: 02392 855330
Email: enquiries@downsed.org
Website: www.downsed.org

Aims to help people with Down's Syndrome achieve more in all areas of their development. It achieves this by informing progress through research and education. Identifies and evaluates interventions that promote the education and development of children with Down's Syndrome. Its education activities (including books, websites, DVDs, teaching materials and training courses) ensure that its evidence-based advice, information and guidance are communicated widely. Also provides early intervention services.

The Dyscovery Centre
University of Wales, Newport
Allt-yr-yn Campus
Newport NP20 5DA
Tel: 01633 432330
Email: dyscoverycentre@newport.ac.uk
Website: www.dyscovery.co.uk

Aims to provide a multi-disciplinary assessment and treatment service on site and home programmes to meet the needs of children with dyspraxia, dyslexia or associated learning difficulties. Provides training courses for professionals and publications, e.g. 'Dyspraxia – Diagnosis in the Pre-school Child, Dyspraxia – Play Activities for the Pre-school Child'.

Dyspraxia Foundation
8 West Alley
Hitchin
Herts SG5 1EG
Tel: 01462 455016
Helpline: 01462 454986
Email: dyspraxia@dyspraxiafoundation.org.uk
Website: www.dyspraxiafoundation.org.uk

Aims to support individuals with dyspraxia and their families. Acts as an information and resource centre, offering support and advice to parents. Promotes rapid diagnosis and treatment and a wider understanding especially among health and education professionals. Produces a range of articles, leaflets and booklets including 'Living with Dyspraxia – Handy Tips', 'Children with Developmental Dyspraxia: Information for Parents/Teachers'.

Elizabeth Foundation
Southwick Hill Road
Cosham
Portsmouth PO6 3LL
Tel: 02392 372735
Email: info@elizabeth-foundation.org
Website: www.elizabeth-foundation.org

For hearing impaired children and their parents, operating from centres in Hampshire and West Yorkshire. Focuses on listening and spoken language skills, music and activities to promote good cognitive skills. Programmes delivered at the centres and also via a national home learning scheme. Support for parents of pre-school children is a priority.

Epilepsy Action
New Anstey House
Gate Way Drive
Yeadon
Leeds LS19 7YY
Helpline: 0808 800 5050
Tel: 0113 210 8800
Email: helpline@epilepsy.org.uk
Website: www.epilepsy.org.uk

Offers a range of services to people with epilepsy including advice and information, a branch network and volunteer scheme. Produces a range of leaflets including 'Epilepsy and Children', 'Epilepsy and Swimming' and DVDs on treatment and first aid.

The Foundation for Conductive Education
Cannon Hill House
Russell Road
Moseley
Birmingham B13 8RD
Tel: 0121 449 1569
Website: www.conductive-education.org.uk

Offers a parent and child service for 0–3s and an early years group for children aged 3+ with cerebal palsy and other neurological disorders. Uses the principles of conductive education.

Henshaws Society for Blind People
John Derby House
88–92 Talbot Road
Old Trafford
Manchester M16 0GS
Tel: 0161 872 1234
Email: info@hsbp.co.uk
Website: www.henshaws.org.uk

Henshaws Children and Family Service supports families and children who have difficulties with their vision. Aims to offer services to families and organize activities throughout the year to ensure there is a good network of support for everyone.

I CAN
8 Wakley Street
London EC1V 7QE
Tel: 0845 225 4073 (information)

Tel: 0845 225 4071 (office)
Email: info@ican.org.uk
Website: www.ican.org.uk

Children's communication charity. Works to support the development of speech, language and communication skills in all children with a special focus on those who find this hard: children with a communication disability.

IPSEA: Independent Panel for Special Education Advice

6 Carlow Mews
Woodbridge
Suffolk IP12 1EA
Adviceline: 0800 018 4016
Tribunal Support Service: 01394 384711
Website: www.ipsea.org.uk

Offers free and independent advice and support to parents of children with special educational needs, including advice on the local authority's legal duties and home visits where necessary. Offers support and possible representation for those parents appealing to the Special Educational Needs Tribunal and second opinions on a child's needs and the provision required.

ISEA: Independent Special Education Advice (Scotland)

164 High Street
Dalkeith
Midlothian EH22 1AY
Tel: 0131 454 0144
Email: advocacy@isea.org.uk
Website: www.isea.org.uk

As above, but for Scotland.

Limbless Association

Roehampton Rehabilitation Centre
Roehampton Lane
London SW15 5PN
Tel: 020 8788 1777
Email: enquiries@limbless-association.org
Website: www.limbless-association.org

Provides information and advice for those who have been born without upper or lower limbs or who have had amputations. Organizes a nationwide network offering support and encouragement. Sponsors research and development in rehabilitation services and limb technology. Produces a quarterly magazine. Has a disability sports section.

LOOK, National Federation of Families with Visually Impaired Children
Queen Alexandra College
49 Court Oak Road
Harborne
Birmingham B17 9TG
Tel: 0121 428 5038
Email: office@look-uk.org
Website: www.look-uk.org

Provides support and information for families of visually impaired children through local groups. Publishes a quarterly newsletter plus access to information on issues such as education, benefits and equipment.

Makaton Vocabulary Development Project
31 Firwood Drive
Camberley
Surrey GU15 3QD
Tel: 01276 61390
Email: mvdp@makaton.org
Website: www.makaton.org

Makaton is a communication system using the spoken word and signs and symbols. Created for children and adults with learning difficulties, it enables people to communicate and encourages language development through visual approach. Has a mail order catalogue of publications including books of the signs and symbols, a Parent Carer Makaton Distance Training Pack plus the signed Nursery Rhyme video with Dave Benson Phillips, Something Special DVDs and more. Organizes workshops on Makaton given by accredited teachers. Family advisory support available.

Mencap
4 Swan Courtyard
Coventry Road
Birmingham B26 1BU
Tel: 0121 707 7877
Minicom: 0808 808 81881
Helpline: 0808 808 1111
Email: help@mencap.org.uk
Website: www.mencap.org.uk

For adults and children with learning disabilities. Offers help and advice on issues such as benefits and can signpost to other organizations. Provides information and support for leisure, recreational services (Gateway clubs), residential services and holidays.

Muscular Dystrophy Campaign

61 Southwark Street
London SE1 0HL
Tel: 020 7803 4800
Helpline: 0800 652 6352
Email: info@muscular-dystrophy.org
Website: www.muscular-dystrophy.org

Focuses on all muscle diseases and provides practical, medical and emotional support to those affected. Provides support through a dedicated Information and Support Service, a network of clinic based Care Advisers, 60 local branches and free publications on topics such as new diagnosis, physiotherapy, housing adaptations and sibling support. Provides grants towards essential equipment through the Joseph Patrick Trust.

National Association of Toy and Leisure Libraries: Play Matters

68 Churchway
London NW1 1LT
Tel: 020 7255 4600
Email: admin@playmatters.co.uk
Website: www.natll.org.uk

National body for toy and leisure libraries in UK. Toy libraries provide good quality carefully chosen toys for young children and often include more specialist toys for those with special needs. They offer a supportive befriending service to parents and carers. Contact Helpline Services at above address for details of your nearest toy library. Has a mail order catalogue of publications on play and special needs.

National Autistic Society

393 City Road
London EC1V 1NE
Tel: 020 7833 2299
Helpline: 0845 070 4004
Email: nas@nas.org.uk
Website: www.autism.org.uk

Provides information, advice and support for those with autism and their families via the Helpline which can also give details of local support and send out information on key issues. Members receive a quarterly newsletter and access to publications, conferences and events. Local branches also offer information and support.

National Blind Children's Society

Bradbury House
Market Street
Highbridge
Somerset TA9 3BW
Tel: 01278 764764

Email: enquiries@nbcs.org.uk
Website: www.nbcs.org.uk

Provides services for the families of children and young people with a visual impairment. Provides family support, educational advocacy, IT advice and support, activities and CustomEyes large print children's books. Subject to criteria, it may be able to provide grants for computers, speech and magnification software for home use.

National Children's Bureau
8 Wakley Street
London EC1V 7QE
Tel: 020 7843 6000
Email: library@ncb.org.uk
Website: www.ncb.org.uk

Promotes the voices, interests and wellbeing of children and young people across every aspect of their lives. Provides information on policy, research and best practice. Also houses the Children's Play Information Service, a library and database on all aspects of children's play.

National Deaf Children's Society
15 Dufferin Street
London EC1Y 8UR
Tel: 020 7490 8656
Helpline: 0808 800 8880 (10–5, Monday–Friday)
Email: ndcs@ndcs.org.uk
Website: www.ndcs.org.uk

Aims to reduce the barriers faced by deaf children. An organization for families, parents and carers providing emotional and practical support through the helpline, a network of trained support workers, a wide range of support services, publications and a website.

National Portage Association
Email: npa@portageuk.freeserve.co.uk
Website: www.portage.org.uk

For parents and professionals who use Portage. The NPA oversees registered Portage services nationally, setting a Code of Practice for the delivery of Portage. NPA provides and monitors training, holds an annual conference and produces a newsletter.

National Society for Epilepsy
Chalfont St Peter
Bucks SL9 0RJ
Tel: 01494 601300
Helpline: 01494 601400 (10–4, Monday–Friday)
Website: www.epilepsynse.org.uk

Provides services for people with epilepsy including medical, social and healthcare and information and support services for anyone affected by epilepsy. Provides a range of publications and materials as well as a helpline.

NCH Action for Children
85 Highbury Park
London N5 1UD
Tel: 020 7704 7000
Website: www.nch.org.uk

Helps children reach their full potential. Supports the most vulnerable and excluded children and young people. Runs a range of services including 60 specialist services for disabled children and their families including short breaks and activity schemes.

Network 81
1–7 Woodfield Terrace
Stansted
Essex CM24 8AJ
Tel: 0870 770 3306 (10–2, Monday–Friday)
Email: network81@btconnect.com
Website: www.network81.org

Offers practical help and support to parents throughout all stages of assessment and statementing as outlined in the Education Act 1996 and Code of Practice 2001. Produces a range of literature including a useful Parents Guide. Also runs training courses for parents and those working with them.

Pyramid Educational Consultants UK Ltd
Pavilion House
6/7 Old Steine
Brighton BN1 1EJ
Tel: 01273 609555
Email: pyramid@pecs.org.uk
Website: www.pecs.org.uk

For information about PECS (Picture Exchange Communication System).

Reach (Association for Children with Hand or Arm Deficiency)
PO Box 54
Helston TR13 8WD
Tel: 0845 130 6225
Email: reach@reach.org.uk
Website: www.reach.org.uk

For families of children with upper limb problems and professionals. Provides information, advice and support and publications including a quarterly newsletter. Also offers access to other families in similar situations.

Rett Syndrome Association UK
113 Friern Barnet Road
London N22 3EU
Tel: 0870 770 3266 Local callers 020 8361 5161
Email: info@rettsyndrome.org.uk
Website: www.rettsyndrome.org.uk

Provides information, advice and support for families of people with Rett Syndrome through a magazine, support groups and a family weekend.

Riding for the Disabled Association
Lavinia Norfolk House
Avenue R
Stoneleigh Park
Kenilworth
Warwicks CV8 2LY
Tel: 0845 658 1082
Website: www.riding-for-disabled.org.uk

Governing body for the Riding for the Disabled Groups around the country. Puts parents in touch with local branches.

Royal Association for Disability and Rehabilitation (RADAR)
12 City Forum
250 City Road
London EC1V 8AF
Tel: 020 7250 3222
Tel: (minicom) 020 7250 4119
Email: radar@radar.org.uk
Website: www.radar.org.uk

Campaigns to promote equality for all disabled people.

Royal National Institute for the Blind (RNIB)
105 Judd Street
London WC1H 9NE
Tel: 020 7388 1266
Helpline: 0845 766 9999
Website: www.rnib.org.uk

For visually impaired people, their families and those who work with them. Offers a wide range of services through its helpline, website and publications.

SCOPE
PO Box 833
Milton Keynes MK12 5NY
Helpline: 0808 800 3333
Email: response@scope.org.uk

Website: www.scope.org.uk

Offers services for people with cerebral palsy and their families including information and advice through a helpline and parent information leaflets, a library and an assessment service. Has local groups and a network of fieldworkers. Has a Schools for Parents scheme to teach parents how to help their child based on conductive education principles.

Sense (The National Deafblind and Rubella Association)
11–13 Clifton Terrace
London N4 3SR
Tel: 0845 127 0060
Text: 0845 127 0062
Email: enquiries@sense.org.uk
Website: www.sense.org.uk

Supports and campaigns for the deafblind and their families. Runs a network of family centres, regional advisory services and branches. Trains Intervenors to work one-on-one to help children and adults develop and explore the world. Offers specialist assessment, nursery and school support, training for parents and help with statementing. Publishes its own magazines and has a booklist which includes 'Deafblind Infants and Children: A Developmental Guide'.

Sensory Integration Network
26 Leopardstown Grove
Blackrock
Co. Dublin
Ireland
Email: info@sensoryintegration.org.uk
Website: www.sensoryintegration.org.uk

Aims to promote research, education and good practice in sensory integration.

Sibs
Meadowfield
Oxenhope
W Yorks BD22 9JD
Tel: 01535 645453
Email: info@sibs.org.uk
Website: www.sibs.org.uk

Sibs is the UK organization for people who grow up with a brother or sister with a disability or chronic illness. Provides information and support to siblings and their families through a helpline, website and workshops. Also trains professionals to run sibling groups.

The Signalong Group
Stratford House
Waterside Court
Rochester
Kent ME2 4NZ
Tel: 0870 7743752
Email: info@signalong.org.uk
Website: www.signalong.org.uk

Signalong is a sign-supporting system based on British Sign Language and designed to help children and adults with communication difficulties, mostly due to learning disabilities or autism. Publications include signing manuals and activity books, CDs and a nursery rhyme video. Training at different levels is provided by a national network of tutors. Information and publications are available through the website.

Speech, Language and Hearing Centre
1–5 Christopher Place
Chalton Street
London NW1 1JF
Tel: 020 7383 3834
Email: info@speech-lang.org.uk
Website: www.speech-lang.org.uk

For children under five with a hearing impairment, communication delay or autism. Offers assessment and therapy, support and guidance for parents and a nursery curriculum and therapy or clinical therapy sessions from an interdisciplinary team.

TEACCH: Treatment and Education of Autistic and Related Communication-handicapped Children
Division TEACCH Administration and Research
CB 7180
The University of North Carolina at Chapel Hill
Chapel Hill
North Carolina 27599–7180
USA
Tel: 001 919 966 2174
Email: TEACCH@unc.edu
Website: www.teacch.com

TEACCH is a service for children with autism offering a structured approach and using visual supports, e.g. timetables. Offers training and publications worldwide.

VisionAid
106 Junction Road
Deane
Bolton BL3 4NE

Tel: 01204 64265
Email: visionaiduk@aol.com
Website: www.visionaid.org.uk

Established by a group of parents to provide advice, information and support for visually impaired children, their families and professionals. Services include an information and reference library, specialist toy loan and visual stimulation equipment, hi-tech aid and tactile photocopying. A helpline is available for information and support and guidance can be given on such issues as education and benefits.

Suppliers of toys and equipment for children with special needs

Often the best places to find novel and eye-catching toys are car boot sales and cheap budget shops. However, there are many fantastic toys available in the high street and through mail order and the internet. For more specialist suppliers of equipment contact the voluntary organization relevant to your child's disability or The Disabled Living Foundation.

Mail order

Galt Educational
Johnsonbrook Road
Hyde
Cheshire SK14 4QT
Tel: 08451 20 30 05
Email: enquiries@galt-educational.co.uk
Website: www.galt-educational.co.uk

Wide range of toys, games and furniture.

Hope Education
Hyde Buildings
Ashton Road
Hyde
Cheshire S14 4SH
Tel: 0845 1202055
Email: enquiries@hope-education.co.uk
Website: www.hope-education.co.uk

Toys and equipment for children including those with special needs (includes fibre-optics).

NES Arnold
Hyde Buildings
Ashton Road
Hyde
Cheshire SK14 4SA
Tel: 0845 1204525
Email: enquiries@nesarnold.co.uk
Website: www.nesarnold.co.uk

Supplies a wide range of toys and equipment.

Nottingham Rehab Supplies
Findel House
Excelsia Road
Ashby de la Zouch
Leics LE65 1NG
Tel: 0845 1204522
Website: www.nrs-uk.co.uk

Provides a mail order catalogue, Ways and Means, of household products for people with special needs. Includes cutlery and crockery, special scissors and pencil grips. Also has a paediatric catalogue with equipment, games and toys for children with special needs.

ROMPA
Goyt Side Road
Chesterfield
Derbyshire S40 2PH
Tel: 01246 221802
Email: sales@rompa.co.uk
Website: www.rompa.co.uk

Supplies mail order toys, soft play and multi-sensory equipment for children with special needs.

TFH Special Needs Toys
5–7 Severnside Business Park
Stourport on Severn
Worcs DY13 9HT
Tel: 01299 827820
Website: www.specialneedstoys.com

Provides a mail order catalogue of fun toys and games for children and adults with special needs.

Winslow
Goyt Side Road
Chesterfield

Derbyshire S40 2PH
Tel: 0845 230 2777
Email: sales@winslow-cat.com
Website: www.winslow-cat.com

Supplies games, books, computer programmes and equipment for children with special needs

Web-based suppliers

www.acorneducational.co.uk
Educational toys and games for children with special needs

www.cheeky-cherub.co.uk
Toys for disabled children

www.eduplayuk.com
Wooden toys

www.fledglings.org.uk
Toys and equipment for disabled children

www.forestbooks.com
Books and DVDs about BSL and deaf issues

www.hobbycraft.co.uk
Arts and crafts materials

www.sensetoys.com
Educational toys and games for children with special needs

www.smartstart-toys.co.uk
Educational and wooden toys

www.special-needs-kids.co.uk
Information directory and shopping site

www.toys-to-you.co.uk
Affordable ethical toys

References

Bruner, J. (1983) Child Talk. Oxford: Oxford University Press.

Bruner, J. (1990) Acts of Meaning. Cambridge, MA: Harvard University Press.

Cooper, J., Moodley, M. and Reynell, J. (1978) Helping Language Development. London: Arnold.

Cribbin, V., Lynch, H., Bagshawe, B. and Chadwick, K. (2003) Sensory Integration Information Booklet. Blackrock, Co Dublin: Sensory Integration Network, UK.

Cunningham, C.E, Reuler, E., Blackwell, J. and Deck, J. (1981) 'Behavioural and linguistic developments in the interaction of normal and retarded children with their mothers.' Child Development 52, 62–70.

Frost, L.A. and Bondy, A.S. (1994) PECS The Picture Exchange Communication System Training Manual. Cherry Hill, NJ: Pyramid Educational Consultants Inc.

Gray, C. and Leigh White, A. (eds) (2002) My Social Stories Book. London: Jessica Kingsley Publishers.

Holmes, J. (1993) John Bowlby and Attachment Theory. London: Routledge.

Jones, O.H.M. (1977) 'Mother–child Communication with Pre-linguistic Down Syndrome and Normal Infants.' In R. Schaffer (ed.) Studies in Mother–Infant Interaction. London: Academic Press.

Law, J. (1994) Before School: A Handbook of Approaches to Intervention with Pre-school Language Impaired Children. London: AFASIC.

Nadel, J. and Camaioni, L. (eds) (1993) New Perspectives in Early Communication Development. London: Routledge.

Piaget, J. (1953) The Origins of Intelligence in the Child. London: Routledge and Kegan Paul.

Polke, L. and Thompson, M. (eds) (1994) Sleep and Settling Problems in Young Children. Southampton: Southampton Community NHS Trust, Child and Family Guidance Service for the Under Fives.

RNIB and Play Matters/NATLL (1987) Look and Touch. London: RNIB.

Sheridan, M.D. (1977) Spontaneous Play in Early Childhood. London: Routledge.

Sime, M. (1980) Read Your Child's Thoughts: Pre-School Learning Piaget's Way. London: Thames and Hudson.

Smith, C.A. with Fluck, M.J. (2001) Scheme to Promote Early Interactive Conversations. A Developmental Scheme to Establish Pre-Linguistic Interpersonal Processes Involved in Sharing a Conversation for Children with Difficulties in Acquiring the Ability to Communicate. Portsmouth: University of Portsmouth.

Sonksen, P.M. (1983) 'Vision and Early Development.' In K. Wybar and D. Taylor (eds) Paediatric Ophthalmology: Current Aspects. New York: Marcel Dekker.

Sonksen, P.M. (1984) 'A developmental approach to sensory disabilities in early childhood.' International Rehabilitation Medicine 7, 27–32.

Sonksen, P.M. and Levitt, S. (1984) 'Identification of constraints acting on motor development in young, physically disabled children and principles of remediation.' Child Care, Health and Development 10, 273–286.

Streeter, E. (1993) Making Music with the Young Child with Special Needs. London: Jessica Kingsley Publishers.

Wells, G. (1985) Language Development in the Pre-School Years. Cambridge: Cambridge University Press.

Williams, M.S. and Schellenberger, S. (1994) How Does Your Engine Run? A Leaders Guide to the Alert Programme for Self-Regulation. Alberquerque, NM: TherapyWorks Inc.

Winnicott, D.W. (1971) Playing and Reality. London: Routledge.

INDEX